蛇龜宅鎮

The tortoise and snake represent the struggle between yin and yang, while the tortoise has inscribed upon its shell the eight trigrams and the constellations of Chinese astrology.

PHOTO: EGIL KORSNES, VESTLANDSKE
KUNSTINDUSTRIMUSEUM, BERGEN.

I CHING

High on Ch'i Shan would have been the oracle temple of the Chou, similar in appearance to this classic depiction.

I CHING

The Shamanic Oracle of Change

Translated by Martin Palmer
and Jay Ramsay,
with Zhao Xiaomin

Calligraphy by Kwok Man Ho

Thorsons
An Imprint of HarperCollins*Publishers*

Thorsons
An Imprint of HarperCollins*Publishers*
77–85 Fulham Palace Road
Hammersmith, London W6 8JB
1160 Battery Street
San Francisco, California 94111–1213

Published by Thorsons 1995

10 9 8 7 6 5 4 3 2 1

© ICOREC 1995
© Calligraphy Kwok Man Ho

A catalogue record for this book
is available from the British Library

ISBN 1 85538 416 7

Background illustrations by Fan Weiming

Printed in Great Britain by Scotprint Ltd,
Musselburgh, Edinburgh

CONTENTS

ACKNOWLEDGEMENTS

Many people have assisted us in our work on this translation and exploration. Susan Mears first saw the possibilities and Glenn Storhaug of Five Seasons Press helped give them shape. In China, friends and colleagues from Beijing and Xian hunted down references and visited sites for us and from their labours came the first insights of the epic. In London, the staff of the library at the School of Oriental and African Studies were as ever a fount of wisdom, not least in helping us find our way through the book stacks!

From Jay's side, special thanks to Carole Bruce, Lucy Lidell, Keith MacNider, Jan Angelo, Katherine Pierpoint, Michael Travers, Ann Carruthers, Alan Jackson, Lindsay Clarke, Annie Wilson, and Bob Moore in Denmark . . . not forgetting the Invisible Ones.

From Martin's side, special thanks to Jo O'Brien, Jo Edwards and Liz Breuilly for their unstinting willingness to be critical!

Finally, an enormous thank you to our editor, Liz Puttick, whose enthusiasm and personal interest in the discoveries we have made have encouraged us throughout, making her more of a companion than just an editor.

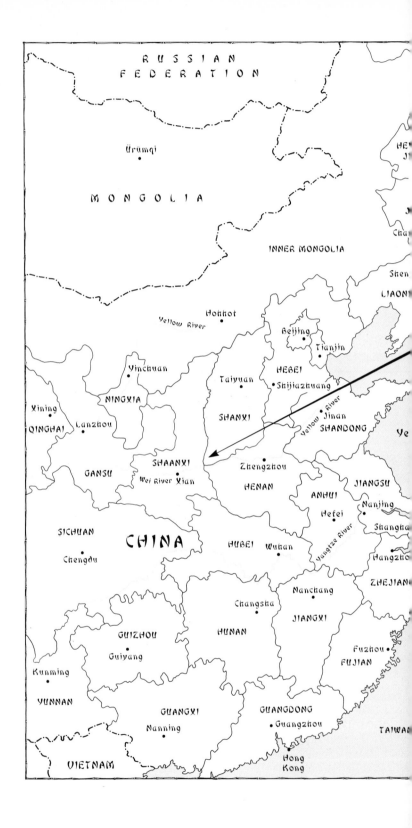

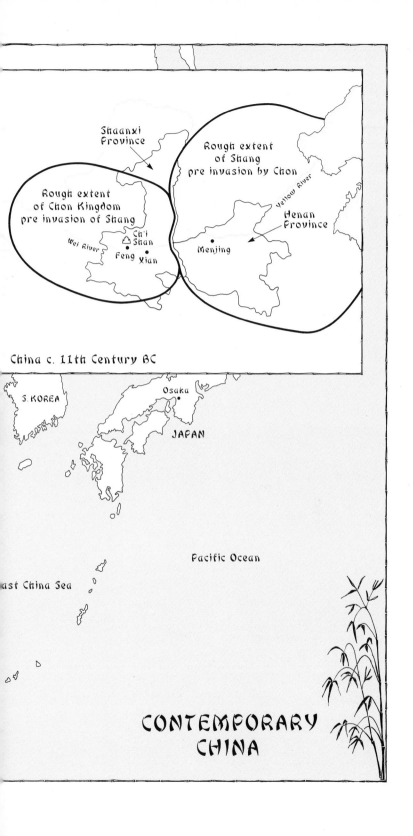

Shaanxi
Province

Rough extent
of Shang
pre invasion by Chon

Rough extent
of Chon Kingdom
pre invasion of Shang

Yellow River

Henan
Province

Wei River

Ch'i
Shan

Feng Xian

Menjing

China c. 11th Century BC

S. KOREA

Osaka

JAPAN

Pacific Ocean

East China Sea

CONTEMPORARY
CHINA

INTRODUCTION

Martin Palmer

DISCOVERING THE *I CHING*

For more than 3,000 years the *I Ching* has been revered as a guide to the development of wisdom for both the individual and the wider community. It has spoken in diverse ways to the Chinese down the years, affecting their culture, art, philosophy, religion and even history. But for centuries a key component of the power and majesty of the *I Ching* has lain hidden and lost. As the West has discovered in recent years, the *I Ching* speaks of the human condition of each individual who turns to it for advice, guidance and inspiration. Yet the very texts that form the heart of the book, the ancient descriptions of each hexagram, have confounded people with their apparent obscurity and randomness.

Now, for the first time since probably the seventh or eighth century BC, the text can be understood in its fullness. Through research in China, archaeological discoveries around Chinese sacred mountains and asking literary, philosophical and historical questions of the text, we have discovered that the ancient text is far from being a random selection of sayings. The *I Ching* is an epic, a saga, which can be compared in significance, both historically and spiritually, with the Exodus experience of the Israelites, the Trojan Wars or the flight to Medina of Muhammad. It is a tale of an oppressed people rising against a tyrant; of the difficulties of leadership and of friendship; of battles and peace; of conquest and corruption; and of the lone voice of the dissenter speaking against the rise of a new oppressor. It is, in other words, the epic of a people's struggle that finds a parallel in the lives of many down the ages, both at a personal level and at a wider social, political and religious level.

But it is even more than this. The *I Ching* echoes the voice of the shaman and the oracle. Again, through the explorations and investigations undertaken for this translation, we have returned to its roots – to a cloudy mountain top in Shensi province, China, where, over 3,000 years ago, a mighty oracle spoke and from its utterances came the origins of the *I Ching*. Today, the voice of the shaman, of one in tune with nature, able to communicate with the natural forces, is once again being heard. The ancient oracles revealed in western China 1,000 years and more before Christ speak today as forcefully to the human condition as they have done throughout the entire history of ancient China. This is the perennial fascination of the *I Ching*, its timelessness. What we can now understand is that it springs from a specific time and place in history, when vast forces collided and fates were sealed, all on the guidance of the shaman oracles of a sacred mountain.

The journey we now want to take you on combines archaeology with personal quest, brings the past and the future into focus, and unites the individual seeker of today with the shamans and leaders of the ancient past. It is both a personal journey of discovery and an epic of the rise of a people. It is truly sacred history.

THE EPIC OF THE *I CHING*

From the very beginning of working on this translation, we decided to go back to the earliest meanings of the Chinese characters. A previous translation of the *I Ching* produced by us at ICOREC in 1985 had done the reverse. Then we had looked at the most contemporary understandings of the *I Ching*, as found amongst the Chinese practitioners of today. In doing so, we had deliberately sought to shake off the confusing, arcane language of translations such as Wilhelm's, which Joseph Needham the great sinologist has aptly described as belonging to the 'Department of Utter Confusion'.

This time, we decided to go back in time. We wanted to discover what each character would have meant at the time it was first used in the text. We wanted to go back over 3,000 years, cutting through later developments of meaning which accrued around each character, to hear as clearly as possible the original message of the text. In doing this we were greatly assisted by studies such as Kwang's *Shang Civilisation* and the

pioneer work of Richard A. Kunst in his PhD work,
The Original 'Yi Jing'.

We were also assisted by colleagues in Xian who were
associated with the historical sites and by the wealth of
information they gave us on recent digs. In looking for the
earliest meanings, we combined a mixture of archaeology
and literary detective work. But most of all it required an
understanding of where the texts had come from in the first
place. By what process had they arisen?

The key to the answer has been provided in the last few
decades by systematic study of the oracle bones of ancient
China. The story of their discovery and their significance is
in itself interesting.

In 1899, the scholar Liu Eh was visiting his friend and fellow
scholar Wang Yi-Jung in Peking. Wang fell ill and, for part of
his treatment, he was prescribed 'dragon bones' to be crushed
as part of a medicine. When Liu Eh looked closely at the
dragon bones, he was astonished to find they had characters
inscribed upon them. But these were not ordinary characters.
They were arcane forms. It was obvious to both scholars that
they had stumbled upon a major discovery. Gradually, and not
without considerable opposition, they began to track down
where the 'dragon bones' had come from. The merchants who
supplied the traditional Chinese medicine shops were worried
by the interest of the scholars and sought to prevent them
from finding out their provenance. But over a number of years,
aided by an increasing number of scholars and interested
parties, the dragon bones were tracked down to a site at
An-yang, Honan. Here, mounds and mounds of the inscribed
bones were unearthed, along with the remains of what was
obviously a major city site dating back to the Shang dynasty
(*c.*1600–1028 BC).

In 1928, systematic excavation began at An-yang and the
inscribed bones began to be deciphered. What had emerged early
on was that the bones were used in oracle ceremonies. These
had been known in theory for centuries. What had not been
realized was how extensive and all-embracing the use of oracle
bones had been in directing the life of the Court and country.

There are two types of oracle bones. The most auspicious is the turtle or tortoise shell. The more common form is the shoulder blade of an ox. In both cases the method of consulting is the same. A question would be posed to the oracle bone. Then indentations would be made on the underside of the shell or bone and a heated stick applied to the indentation. As the heat rose through the shell or bone, it produced cracks on the upper surface. These were then 'read' and if the oracular pronouncement proved to be auspicious (or inauspicious but nevertheless true), the characters discerned in the cracks were inscribed upon the shell or bone as a record. Here are two fairly typical examples:

> *Enquiry of the date* yi mao. *Enquiry, the king wishes to hunt today, will he be prevented by strong winds? Answer. There will be strong winds.*
>
> QUOTED IN *CHINA IN ANTIQUITY* BY HENRI MASPERO, P.26, UNIVERSITY OF MASSACHUSETTS PRESS, 1978.

> *P'an Keng wanted to move his capital to Yin, but the people would not follow him there. So he summoned before him all those who opposed and grumbled and spoke to them, saying, 'Our king came and he himself founded this city. He did so because he cared deeply for the people. I love my people and cannot stand back and watch them perish in a place where they are unable to defend themselves. Therefore I have consulted the oracle and have received the answer, "This place is not good for you." '*
>
> *SHU CHING*, PART IV, BOOK 7, PART 1, VERSE 2, OUR TRANSLATION.

Judging by the scale of oracle bone finds in An-yang (thought to be over 100,000), the Shang dynasty resorted to them on numerous occasions. Nor were they alone in this, for the practice seems to have been very widespread. Its significance for the *I Ching* is that the most ancient sections of it are beyond doubt oracle bone texts.

We now need to turn to another strand in the journey of the *I Ching*. This strand links in with the oracle bones, and in a most interesting way, for it is the story of invasion and migration that brought down a mighty dynasty and sparked the very origins of the *I Ching*.

THE STORY OF THE CHOU TRIBES

The earliest name for the *I Ching* was the *Chou I*, meaning 'The Changes of Chou'. The Chou after whom the book was named were a collection of tribal peoples who originated somewhere in the high mountains to the North West of China. As the fourth century BC Taoist philosopher Chuang Tzu records, they were forced down from these mountains by the encroachment of more barbaric tribes, the ferocious Ti peoples. This migration brought them to Ch'i Shan, a high mountain range, and to the very edge of the lands ruled by the Shang dynasty, around 1325 BC. Chuang Tzu recounts this part of the story:

> *The Great King T'an Fu [of the Chou tribes] lived in Pin and the Ti peoples invaded. He tried to pay them off with skins and silks, but that did not satisfy them. He tried to appease them with dogs and horses, but they did not like that. He offered them pearls and jade, but they were not placated by that for the Ti peoples were only interested in his lands. Great King T'an Fu said, 'To live here with the older brothers and to despatch the younger brothers to death; and to live amongst the fathers and despatch the sons to death, this I cannot do. My children, stay here! Does it really matter whether I rule you or the Ti people do? I have heard people say that you should never use that by which you care for the people, to harm the people.' Then, picking up his staff and riding crop, he left. However the people, all following one another, came after him and soon they founded a new country under Ch'i Mountain. The Great King T'an Fu knew how to care for life.*
>
> CHUANG TZU, CHAPTER 28, OUR TRANSLATION.

The story of the migration of the Chou peoples is also recorded in one of the poems contained within the classic text, the *Shih Ching*, or 'Book of Poetry' (*c.* eighth–fifth century BC). The poem records not just their settling in a new area, but also the use of turtle oracle divination:

> *The ancient duke, T'an Fu,*
> *Early in the morning came galloping upon his horse,*
> *Beside the rivers of the West,*
> *To below Ch'i [mountain].*
> *Here, he and the woman of the Chiang,*
> *Came together and sought a site to settle.*

The plain of Chou looked so rich and beautiful,
Its celery and sowthistle as good as dumplings.
Here we will make a start, here we will seek advice.
Here mark our turtle shell.
It says, 'Stop here.' It says, 'This is the auspicious time.
This is where you shall build your homes.'

SHIH CHING, PART III, BOOK 1, ODE 3, VERSES 2–4,
OUR TRANSLATION.

The Chou peoples settled in the area around Mount
Ch'i – Ch'i Shan, which means the double-peaked mountain –
and soon became a significant presence in the area. Before
long they fell under the suzerainty of the Shang dynasty, but
they maintained their own sense of independence. This was
focused upon two things: their own kings and their ancestral
temple on the sacred mountain Ch'i Shan. The two were
intimately intertwined, for the king was in effect one of the
most senior priests of the cult of the ancestors and of the
sacred mountain, while his role in divination often paralleled
or enhanced that of the Court shaman/diviner.

The sacred mountain Ch'i Shan was the centre of all Chou
courtly and religious life. It is part of a high mountain range
which lies some 100 miles due West of Sian, in Shensi
province. In 1977 excavations at the mountain unearthed
considerable collections of oracle bones, confirming its
importance as a religious and political centre. At the same site
ritual vessels associated with ancestor worship and divination
were also discovered.

What is so interesting about Ch'i Shan and its oracle bones is
that it was here on this mountain top that the *I Ching* began
life as a series of oracles given to the kings of Chou.

THE ORACLE AS EPIC

What we also have uncovered is that these oracles were given
over a very short period of time. Even more significant, they
tell the story of an epic struggle and uprising of the Chou,
which led to the overthrow of the Shang dynasty in the
eleventh century BC. Running through the ancient texts of the
I Ching is an epic which ranks alongside the Exodus or the
siege of Troy.

The clue that set us on the historical path was the phrase 'cross the great river' which appears seven times. For the Chou, living West of the Yellow River, the 'great river' is none other than the Yellow River itself. This vast river was both a physical barrier with the Shang empire and a mental barrier. To cross the great river meant to break out of the mountains and into the fertile plains. Thus crossing the great river means to undertake a vast enterprise – the conquest of Shang, no less.

Alongside this clue were the various oracles which spoke of the difficulties of forging some sort of an alliance – texts such as Hexagram 2, which talks of having 'friends in the South West and losing friends in the North East', or Hexagram 11, in which the 'lesser ones leave and the great come', only to be followed in Hexagram 12 with 'the great leave and the lesser ones come.'

It was also clear that the text builds up to a climax of expectation around Hexagram 30, traditionally the last hexagram in section one of the *I Ching*. Thereafter, the oracles deal not so much with some vast undertaking which everyone has to be drawn into but with the aftermath or consequences of such an undertaking.

The question which we started with was why would the Chou have preserved these particular oracles, given the tens of thousands, if not hundreds of thousands, of oracles which they would have consulted. What was so special about these? In the past it has been assumed that they were collected over hundreds of years as pieces of wisdom. Yet they actually spell out a story-line – not in conventional fashion, for they were, after all, oracle readings which in many cases forecast or encouraged actions which then followed – but they do record the progression of a major undertaking: the invasion of the Shang dynasty by the Chou tribes. The reason these oracles were collected together, and known for some 800 years or so as the 'Changes of Chou', is quite simply that they are the oracles which led the Chou to rise against oppression. They are in effect a sort of Bayeux Tapestry of China in words. Furthermore, this extraordinary text not only chronicles the invasion but also deals with the problems which then beset the victorious army and people, and ends by posing questions of power and corruption in ways not dissimilar to Greek tragedy or the spirit of the *Iliad*.

It has long been known that the Chou celebrated their victory over the Shang once a year at their ancestral temple. Ritual dances re-enacted the conquest and it would seem fair to now speculate that the oracles associated with the invasion were also annually recalled and recited, leading to the compilation of at least part of what we now know as the *I Ching*. This is very similar to the role that some of the Psalms had when they were used to celebrate Israel's victories and conquest and were annually recited in the Temple, or the Norse tradition of bards composing epic sagas to be sung at feasts, recalling the triumphs of the warriors.

The Beginning of the *I Ching* – the Oracles are Given

The story of which we have so far just given hints starts with the accession of the last ruler of the Shang dynasty, Emperor Chou. Renowned for his physical prowess, he was very cunning but also violent. His personal life-style was one of excess and extravagance. It is customary for last rulers of dynasties to be depicted as debauched despots by those who overthrow them and no doubt there is something of this in the stories associated with Emperor Chou. However, there are enough specific instances to show that he was not a terribly pleasant person.

For example, his wild life-style caused his uncle, Prince Pi Kan, to rebuke him, complaining that Emperor Chou's abuse of power and finances was ruining the country. Emperor Chou's response was to say, 'It is said that you are a sage and that sages have seven openings to their hearts. I want to see if this is true.' With that he ordered that his uncle's heart be cut out.

The excesses which Prince Pi Kan was protesting about were often linked to Emperor Chou's favourite consort, Ta Chi. In order to impress her, he created vast lakes filled with wine and hung fresh meat from trees to create a meat forest. With such activities he wasted the financial and manpower resources of his country.

In another story frequently told, Emperor Chou was travelling one day when he espied farmers knee deep in cold water, planting crops. He was convinced that their legs must be different from ordinary legs to enable them to withstand the cold and wet, so to find out he ordered the farmers out of the water and had their legs cut off.

Most infamous as far as the *I Ching* is concerned is Emperor Chou's imprisonment of King Wen of the Chou. This venerable old man was locked up for over a year. According to later legend, while he was a prisoner in the Shang dungeons he fell to writing down the 64 basic texts – what we are terming 'oracles' – of the *I Ching*. Clearly this is not the case. Legend, however, wanted to honour him, for he was the father of the eventual conqueror of Emperor Chou, and this was one way of doing it. However, while King Wen did not write the hexagram texts, if our hypothesis is correct, they were given by the oracle just after his death. It is this belief, for different reasons, that Helmut Wilhelm echoes when he says, '...modern Chinese research, which for a long time held widely divergent views as to the time of origin of the *I Ching*, has now come back to placing this stratum of text in the time of King Wen.' (Helmut Wilhelm, *Change: Eight Lectures on the 'I Ching'*, Routledge & Kegan Paul, 1961, p.11)

King Wen was eventually released after he had offered up most of his lands to Emperor Chou in return not just for his own freedom but for agreement from the Emperor that a particularly barbaric torture he had invented be abandoned. This torture, known as the 'Grill Roast Technique', where people were laid on red hot grids and literally roasted, reflects the personal fascination which all accounts portray Emperor Chou as having for cruelty and violence.

Soon after his return to the Chou tribes, King Wen died and his son King Wu ascended the throne. He was a very different sort of character. Aggressive and opportunist, he soon saw that the Shang dynasty was ready to fall. It is he who called for the oracles to be read for advice on whether to attack or not and it is with him that the *I Ching* as such really begins life.

THE DECLINE OF THE SHANG DYNASTY AND THE RISE OF THE CHOU

Evidence of what exactly happened in the dying years of the Shang is scant and flimsy. We have to rely upon histories written centuries later and on odd bits of archaeological evidence. Discerning history from myth in this period is almost impossible. What does seem to emerge, however, is that the Chou tribes felt increasingly oppressed and affronted by the behaviour of Emperor Chou. Indeed, Ssu Ma Ch'ien, the famous historian of China in the first century BC, records that many of the subordinate lords of the Shang grew tired and frightened of Emperor Chou's eclectic behaviour and drifted towards the lands of the Chou. The Chou themselves also seem to have felt that the rich farmlands of the Shang were a desirable objective in their own right.

It is interesting to compare two accounts of the reasons for the overthrow of the Shang. The first comes from the *Shu Ching*, the 'Book of History'. The section called the *Book of Chou* opens thus:

> *In the spring of the thirteenth year there was a great assembly at Mang-tsin. The king said, 'So! Hereditary rulers of our friendly states, and all you my officers, managers of my affairs, listen clearly to my declaration. Heaven and Earth are the parents of all forms of life, and of all these humanity is the most highly endowed. The most sincere, intelligent and perspicacious becomes the First Ruler and is the mother and father of all the people. Now Chou, King of Shang, shows no love to Heaven above nor to the people below. He has abandoned himself to drunkenness and lust; he has become a cruel oppressor. He not only punishes criminals but also their whole family. He gives men positions based upon hereditary claims, and lavishes money on palaces, towers, pavilions, ponds and all manner of other extravagances, and all at terrible cost to you the ordinary people. He has burned and roasted the loyal and good. He has ripped open pregnant women. Lofty Heaven has been moved with indignation and commanded my father, the late King Wen, to enact its revenge, but he died before this could be fulfilled.*

The text goes on to say how he, King Wu, will now take up the challenge and will fight Emperor Chou and overthrow him, thus freeing the people from his oppression. This account is also further filled out in the *Annals of the Bamboo Books*, which describe how Wu brought his hordes to the banks of the Yellow River, at the ford at Mang (now known as Menjing, 20 miles to the North of Luo Yang City in Henan), where his 'eight hundred princes came together'. The crossing of the Yellow River at Mang features in a number of the most ancient texts and we will return to it shortly.

From the *Shu Ching*, the impression is of a noble king setting out to avenge the people and to carry out the commands of Heaven to restore virtue to the world – good epic material and, as much of the 'Book of History' was written down during the Chou dynasty (*c.*1050–770 BC), it almost certainly reflects the sort of heroic image the Chou wanted.

A less flattering version is given by Chuang Tzu, writing after the final collapse of the last remnants of the Chou, *c.*350 BC. He, you will recall, had spoken most movingly of the wisdom of the earlier Chou king T'an Fu, who had moved rather than fight a mighty enemy. It is in this context that the following story needs to be set.

> *Earlier, in the time of the Chou dynasty's triumph, there were two scholars who lived in Ku Chu called Po Yi and Shu Chi. The two said one to another, 'I have heard that in the West there is a man who has the Tao, so let's go and visit him.' When they reached the sunlit side of Mount Ch'i, King Wu heard about them and sent Shu Tan to see them. He suggested they make an agreement, saying, 'Your wealth will be second in rank and your titles of the first rank if you agree to this proposal and seal it with blood and bury it.'*
> *The two friends looked at each other and burst out laughing, saying, 'How odd! This is not what we would call the Tao. In the ancient past Shen Nung had the whole world and he carried out the ritual sacrifices at the appointed times and with great respect, but he never dreamt of praying for blessings. When dealing with people he was true and honest and did what was right, but never expected anything from them. He liked to rule fairly and when necessary would be stern and strict. He did not exploit the failures of others in order to further his own powers. He did not use other people's weakness to increase his own strength. He did not exploit favourable openings in order to make a profit. But now the Chou, seeing the Yin [Shang] have fallen into disarray, suddenly seize the government from them, asking*

advice from the leaders and bribing the ordinary people. It has brought out its weapons and offered sacrifices and made pacts with people to try and show how serious it is. It shouts its own praises in order to impress the people and it attacks just for the sake of gain: this is to overthrow disorder and replace it with tyranny.'

CHAPTER 28, OUR TRANSLATION.

A somewhat less complimentary account, but one which is of importance for understanding the *I Ching*. For the sacrifices which Chuang Tzu refers to at the end are the offerings and sacrifices which the *I Ching* talks about in almost all the hexagrams, and the whole slant of sceptical cynicism about power and violence is one which, despite its status as the oracle record of the invasion, the *I Ching* actually ends with.

It is perhaps this problem of the heroic versus the corrupt which so captures the quixotic nature of the *I Ching*. It is because it casts both a positive as well as a negative or quizzical light on human behaviour and motivations that it has risen beyond just a historical ritual recitation to become a classic of personal journey and discovery. This is something we shall look at in more depth later.

King Wu Consults the Oracle on Ch'i Shan

HEXAGRAMS 1–5

Whatever the reasons for the invasion, sometime in the eleventh century BC (dates vary from 1122 to 1111 to 1027 BC), King Wu of Chou ascended the sacred mountain of Ch'i Shan and consulted the oracles. This is where the *I Ching* begins. The opening five oracles (Hexagrams 1–5) are the first salvoes in both the struggle to conquer the Shang and the struggle between the temporal and spiritual powers which runs as a thread throughout the invasion saga. The first three oracles (Hexagrams 1–3) are almost identical in their opening lines, in that the characters found in Hexagram 1 are repeated in 2 and 3.

The opening text, Hexagram 1, concerns the offering of an original sacrifice, a mighty immolation which brought 'a favourable oracle'. Here is recorded King Wu's initial sacrifice or offering, seeking advice on whether to even start such a scheme as the invasion of Shang. He was obviously pleased with the positive response.

Hexagram 2 repeats the details of the successful offering and favourable reading, but then expands a bit more into giving a good outline of the sorts of problems that the king has to face. It talks of taking initiatives and of how some of these will fail. It urges perseverance until the right way has been found. It also cautions that not all those who will be invited to join the attack will come. It is a wise piece of advice to a leader preparing for a major undertaking. It is also interesting to note that while Wu is known to later history as King Wu, he was probably not considered a king at the time. Indeed, given the polyglot mixture of tribes and leaders (all the ancient historians talk of 800 leaders joining the revolt), he was probably simply the greatest leader – the famous 'great man' of the texts.

The wise advice is continued in Hexagram 3, where again the original successful oracle is repeated. This is followed by cautionary advice.

Hexagram 4 introduces us to something very different. Here, in an extraordinary reading, we have not a third person voice but first person. The oracle speaks in terms of 'I' – and is obviously becoming frustrated! It rebukes those who keep coming to it and who are youthful and shallow. It would appear that the young leader Wu has been pushing it a bit. This strange oracle has a tremendous ring of authenticity about it. You can see the shaman and the oracle getting fed up with the constant requests for more and more favourable readings. The oracle is basically saying, 'Look, I've said it will work, so stop asking about that and get on with it!' In other words, Wu has now been told most definitely that the oracle is on his side, but that he, Wu, must now seize the moment. This sense of a Voice which is beyond and above the simple concerns of the military leader is a vital one to the life of the *I Ching*. We shall look more closely at the role of the shaman later, but what is clear even at this early stage is that while the oracle will support the invasion, it has a mind and an agenda of its own. This, as it will be seen later, essentially subversive role of the oracle is one which turns what otherwise might have been a war chronicle into one of the most powerful texts on the limits of political and military power.

Finally, in Hexagram 5, Wu is given the reading he has been looking for. He is told that if he is confident and makes the right sacrifices, then he can cross the great river. This is the first time the Yellow River is mentioned and given its role as the most serious physical barrier between the two countries. It is clear that when Wu is told to cross the river he is being given authority from Heaven to invade. With this oracle, the conquest is underway.

Forging Alliances

Hexagrams 6–8

However, this is a true drama! For from now on until Hexagram 30, we see the fluctuations, tensions and indecisions which mark any great undertaking. Immediately after the favourable oracle of Hexagram 5 comes a far more cautious one. By now Wu has descended from the mountain top and is probably travelling along the River Wei towards the Yellow River. En route he has to gather to him the various tribes and leaders who will constitute his invasion force. Decisions about tactics and alliances have to be entered into. Life becomes difficult. With him travel the shamans and the oracle bones. In the midst of troubles he turns to the oracle again. Hexagrams 6–8 form a group.

In Hexagram 6 the oracle says, 'Yes, there are difficulties, but do not give up. Be cautious. Not everything that looks good now will work. So draw together around the great man but do not cross the great river yet.' Good advice, for if there are unresolved tensions, this is no time to invade. It reminds one of the debates that took place in the camp of the Greeks before invading Troy or the preparations which William the Conqueror made before launching his invasion of England in AD 1066.

In Hexagram 7 Wu is advised to consolidate the forces he has by the appointment of leaders he can trust.

In Hexagram 8, having found a new unity, he is urged to press ahead, for to delay will bring misfortune. Hiccup number one is over!

Struggle for Power

HEXAGRAMS 9–15

Hexagrams 9–15 form another set of texts dealing with a crisis. Real difficulties have emerged. Suddenly it is not working and we are back to square one. Everyone is wanting to get in on the act and the oracle warns against letting the less important leaders think they are as important as the major leaders.

In Hexagram 9, it also obliquely (as is the wont of oracles) refers to the problem of having certain major leaders who are not whole-heartedly committed. This the oracle describes by saying, 'Heavy clouds come from the West but there is no rain.' In other words, some of the Chou tribes from the far West are making lots of noise, but not offering much in the way of real commitment.

Hexagram 10 sends out a clear warning that things are dangerous with its again oblique references to walking on a tiger's tail. The tiger is a common symbol for a martial Emperor in Chinese tradition. Wu is being advised here to attack the Tiger/Emperor but to do so with due care and preparation!

Hexagram 11 seems optimistic, for significant forces have come and some of the troublesome lesser lords have departed, no doubt offended at being excluded from the sacrifices, as recommended by Hexagram 9. Yet all looks well, but it isn't!

Hexagram 12 tells of revolt. There has been a rebellion and the leader, here referred to as the nobleman, cannot do anything about this. The rebellion seems to have involved some of the major leaders, who were jockeying for power. Again, there are very interesting parallels here with what happened on the First Crusade at the end of the eleventh century AD, when the various princes and nobles of Europe squabbled over who was to be the leader. This is, in other words, a very familiar story.

In Hexagram 13, a solution is found. By now the invading army is on the very edges of the Shang lands, drawing close to the great river, the mighty Yellow River. And it is here, says the oracle, that the leader will find tribes who will join the fight. 'Here on the frontier are your allies,' it says, 'so press ahead and cross the great river.'

This is further backed up by Hexagram 14, which is simply one of great optimism. It urges the army to make a major offering as thanksgiving. After the revolt and disruption, the invasion is on course again.

As a result, says Hexagram 15, the leader is guaranteed success. It evokes the particular qualities of leadership.

Preparing for the Attack

HEXAGRAMS 16–18

Hexagrams 16–18 take us on a step further. By now the invasion force is camped on the Chou side of the Yellow River.

Hexagram 16 tells the leader to establish the commanders for the different parts of the army and to move up ready for the attack.

In 17, the original offering and reading is recalled and reassurance is given that what is happening is what is meant to happen.

In 18, the corruption of the Shang dynasty is evoked by the term 'implosion' and very specific instructions are given about making all the proper preparations for the crossing of the great river. In the *Shu Ching*, the 'Book of History', these preparations and the interest in auspicious auguries are given in great detail.

The Invasion is Underway

HEXAGRAMS 19–26

It is our contention that after Hexagram 18 the invasion is underway, for the next set of texts, Hexagrams 19–26, reflect a time of uncertainty, of reverses of fortune and of preoccupation with ritual. There is a sense of a host who have encountered opposition and difficulties.

Hexagram 19 reminds the leader of the original offering and favourable oracle, but adds that while this remains true, there will be trouble in the eighth month. We see the leader holding the tension within, poised but not yet active.

Hexagrams 20–2 are concerned with what was obviously a major sacrifice, presumably to placate Heaven and win its favour, as the invasion became bogged down.

By 23, the oracle is giving its advice, namely, 'Get out of this fix, never mind where, just move!' 'You have been freed,' it seems to say, 'in order to confront your destiny.'

This is followed by the promise of reinforcements and help in Hexagram 24, though 25 speaks of someone betraying the original vision and of their inevitable failure.

By 26, the invasion is back on course, the tempo is rising and the oracle explains this by using as a metaphor the term 'cross the great river' to mean 'go on with the vast undertaking'.

The Battle is Won

HEXAGRAMS 27–30
From 27 to 30, we see the army redoubling its efforts.

Hexagram 27 is an oracle of comfort and of endurance.

In Hexagram 28 the Chou are told that the House of Shang is about to fall, in the vivid oracle, 'The house is falling down, so go!' In fact the Chinese says that the central beam of the house is twisted, which captures the notion that because of the corruption and debauchery of Emperor Chou, the whole house of Shang is now unstable. A very clear image.

In 29, the leader is told to summon up all his courage and to take the plunge, to make the final push, and in 30, we see that the battle has been won and it is time to make the appropriate offerings of the cow (symbolizing the domestic) and the bull (symbolizing the warlike) in thanksgiving.

Traditionally, the first section of the *I Ching* ends with Hexagram 30. This seems to make sense, for by this time the conquest has taken place in terms of the major battles and struggles. Thereafter, we see a society trying to settle down and make sense of its sudden power and wealth, and we begin to hear the voice of the sceptic, the oracle, which now points beyond the Chou to problems to do with the nature of power itself. The excitement and adventure of the first 30 oracles, as they push and cajole the Chou into undertaking their invasion and overcoming the sorts of problems associated with such a venture, now give way to pettier problems and difficulties.

According to the histories, such as the *Shu Ching* and Ssu Ma Ch'ien's great history the *Shih Chi*, the Chous' conquest of Shang was pretty swift. Ssu Ma Ch'ien's description is as good as any:

> *Thereupon Chou King Wu came to lead his subordinate lords in a conquest of Shang. Ti Chou sent his troops to resist them at Mu Yeh [near present-day Weihui in Henan]. On day* chia-tzu, *Ti Chou's troops were defeated. Emperor Chou went in, climbed the Deer Platform, put on his precious jade clothing, and went into a fire to his death. Chou King Wu cut off Chou's head, hanging it at the top of a large white flag pole.*

Adjusting to Victory

Hexagrams 31–4

From Hexagram 31 onwards we enter a different sort of world, a world in which it is as likely that the enemy is within as without.

Hexagram 31 seems to be concerned with settling the invaders down with wives. Again, there are parallels in the actions of, say, Alexander the Great after he had conquered Persia. He encouraged his officers and soldiers to marry local women and settle down, for they were not going home again.

In 32 we have the oracle being reassuring and confirming settlement.

In 33 we hear again the voice of the oracle. It would appear that after the conquest, people became a little less interested in the oracle and this was being reflected in rather insignificant offerings. The oracle has strong views on this. 'Withholding the offering means little is gained from the oracle!' In other words, 'Don't ignore me just because you have won! Do not disconnect at the very moment when you most need to remain grounded.'

Hexagram 34 confirms this by its terse 'Favourable oracle.' Obviously the army had followed its advice.

Dissension

HEXAGRAMS 35–40

From Hexagram 35 to 40 we see the ups and down of settling a conquered land.

In 35 we hear of the leader subduing and being given gifts by the conquered peoples.

Hexagram 36 shows that problems have surfaced again and he is being advised to learn from difficulties.

Hexagram 37 is a very interesting oracle, for it seems to be urging a return to certain basic values which the conquerors neglect at their peril. The hexagram is called 'The Clan', but this could as easily be translated as the 'tribe' or 'family'. 'Remember your roots,' it says, and mentions the role of the woman shaman. It would appear from studies into ancient Chinese shamanism (of which more later) that originally women were the main shamans. As societies settled and became more paternalistic, men took over until women were virtually excluded from the role they once fulfilled. The oracle is saying, 'Listen to the woman.'

Hexagram 38 urges perspective. Don't get bogged down in minor disagreements and problems – consolidate the major gains of the invasion.

In 39 and 40, troubles are upon the Chou again, and their leader is obviously asking advice about whom he can trust and where to place his troops. We see here the discontent that continues after an invasion and we know from history that often ousted dynasties would continue to put up resistance in more inaccessible regions for years after the initial conquest.

Reassurance from the Oracle

HEXAGRAMS 41–2

In 41, the oracle returns to its desire to reassure but also reminds those who serve it of its needs.

Hexagram 42 seems to be yet further reassurance that the invaders have done the right thing. Again, one can imagine that as the excitement of the conquest died down, people wanted to go home and not be stuck in this foreign land. There are echoes here of the complaints that Moses or Alexander the Great got from their followers when they were tired of the effort necessary to take over a whole land or to make radical moves.

A Warning Voice

HEXAGRAMS 43–4

Hexagram 43 brings us to the beginning of the change. At odd times now we shall hear what is in effect a dissenting voice. Here it appears for the first time. When we were translating this we called this voice the 'Cassandra voice'. Cassandra, you will recall, was the one person who cried out against bringing the Wooden Horse left by the Greeks into the city of Troy. She was sure it was a plot and, of course, was right. But no one wanted to hear her warnings, for they were sure they had triumphed. Well, here is a Chinese Cassandra. The oracle is warning that even though it will be unpopular and ignored, it has to caution that things are on a dangerous edge. 'Don't mix the spiritual with the political.'

Hexagram 44 takes this further. Here the oracle specifically warns against a marriage. But what is interesting is that the reason given is that the woman in question is 'powerful'. Our contention here is that the victorious leader Wu has overstepped the mark and is either wishing to take for a wife someone from the old dynasty or is contemplating marrying a woman shaman, thus combining both ruler and priest/shaman in his new role. This is a very terse oracle and very clear: 'Mingling. The woman is powerful. Do not marry this woman.'

The Ritual of Kingship

HEXAGRAMS 45–50

Perhaps this rebuke came just in time, for in 45 we see a somewhat compliant king coming to make a special offering. And here we see a shift taking place. The great man of the earlier texts is still here but the term is used in conjunction with the word 'king' for the first time. Until now, 'king' has not occurred in these oracle texts. Our contention is that Wu was just the mightiest of a bunch of lords and rulers who rose against the Shang. It was only after the conquest that he became a king, and perhaps the offerings and ritual described here are part of his coronation ceremony. In which case, just as the Pope's crowning of emperors symbolized the authority of the spiritual over the temporal, perhaps the oracle is reasserting its power over the military.

Hexagram 46 takes us on from this major ritual, invoking the original offering made at the start of the campaign, and in this light urging further conquest of the South. Mopping up operations are obviously still going on.

Now we come to further voices of dissension and warnings of not pushing too far.

In 47, we have a hint of dissension. Someone is trying to tell the leader what will be auspicious for him, but he is not listening.

By Hexagram 48 this becomes even more blunt. Using the metaphor of a well, the oracle makes a number of points. First, it points out that even if the rulers or political systems change, the well, symbolizing the basic needs of life, continues unaffected. Secondly, it makes it clear that unless you are properly prepared, you will do more damage than good by rushing into something. Here is the voice of the prophet, reminiscent of the parables and social political messages that the prophets of Israel such as Amos or Hosea employed. 'Be warned, great man,' the oracle is saying. 'Conquest is ephemeral, but life is constant. Power is not all, but proper concern to do things correctly is essential.'

Hexagrams 49 and 50 continue in this vein, urging transformation and invoking the original offering and reading again, only this time as a warning of the need to be changed or face being overthrown. In essence it is saying, 'Look, you've just conquered an entire empire. Relax!'

The Shaman

HEXAGRAMS 51–2

In 51 we meet a character who is without fear. Whether this is the shaman or the king it is hard to say, for he is described as playing a leading role in some ritual, a role which either a shaman or king could have fulfilled. The character, which we have translated as 'trauma', is the one for 'thunder'. We have deliberately given it a wider meaning, for the notion of thunder here seems to mean some great shock. Perhaps we have here the priest/shaman who stands erect and secure even in the midst of the most cataclysmic upheavals, such as a major invasion.

Hexagram 52 casts some light back on 51, for it gives a description of a sage or even of what later would become known as an 'immortal', someone who can centre themselves and who would appear to be able to travel outside the body. Given that much of the language of Taoist immortals and sages which echoes this sort of statement has its roots in shamanism, this may well be a description of the shaman/priest whom we encountered in 51. He is obviously a person of immense powers, but, in contrast to those of the king, they are not military or egotistical.

Caution

HEXAGRAMS 53–4

In 53 and 54 we have a pair of oracles. We are not sure whether these refer to an actual situation or were always meant metaphorically.

In 53 the oracle urges marriage to a woman, but 54 warns against marriage to a younger sister. Our feeling is that, rooted in some historical precedent, these texts refer to making choices between an older, more experienced person and a younger, inexperienced person. This is strengthened by Hexagram 54, where not marrying a younger woman is linked to not pressing ahead with an attack.

Returning Home

With Hexagrams 55–62 we are back on chartable historic ground. These oracles are all concerned with the king making the appropriate offerings at his ancestral temple. The triumphant oracle is going home, back to its distant mountain, Ch'i Shan, its job done. In the *Shu Ching*, we read of exactly such a return home by the victorious Wu:

> *In the fourth month, at the first sighting of the moon, the king came from Shang to Feng [the city on the plains below Ch'i Shan]. There he stopped all the activities of warfare and turned to the activities of peace. He sent his horses back to graze to the South of Hua Shan and released the oxen [used for pulling the war wagons] in the plains of Tao Lin. Thus did he show everyone under Heaven that he would not have need of them again. On the day* ting wei *he sacrificed in the ancestral temple of Chou, when the officers of the imperial realm and of the subordinate states all made offerings of the special dishes. Three days later he made a burnt offering and venerated the mountains and rivers, solemnly announcing the successful end of the war.*
> ADAPTED FROM LEGGE'S TRANSLATION OF PART V, BOOK III, P.3.

In Hexagram 55, we see the king departing for his homeland to make the sacrifice. The actual title of this hexagram, Feng, is the same character as that of the new city founded after the victory and built on the plains below Ch'i Shan.

In 56 we encounter one of those enigmatic figures that the *I Ching* throws up from time to time. This one, to be put alongside the Cassandra figure and the prophet figure, is called 'the traveller'. The Chinese character is interesting, for it does not just signify any old traveller. In later centuries it was the character used to describe a wandering Taoist priest cum magician. This is no travelling salesman, but a powerful, idiosyncratic figure who wanders the world to show his contempt for settled, 'normal' life. It is in this context that his appearance is so significant. Here, at the precise point at which the victorious king returns home, the trappings of a successful war before him, hosts of followers following him, the traveller wanders across his path. We would contend that Hexagrams 56 to 58 concern this figure. His role is to pinprick the assumptions of the king. He is like the figure who rode

beside the victorious Emperors of Rome when they held a
Triumph to celebrate victory over some enemy. His role was to
whisper in the Emperor's ear as the crowds roared their
approval, 'You are but mortal!'

In Hexagram 56 the traveller wanders in. The oracle says that
he makes a small offering, in contrast to the vast immolations
which we know the kings of that time offered – hundreds
upon hundreds of animals. In return the oracle offers the
traveller a blessing of good fortune.

In 57, the small offering is again referred to, and the traveller is
urged to go where he wants to. This uses almost the same
terminology as that used to encourage the army to go where it
has to in attack. But here, in yet another instance of turning
the tables, it is the wandering, footloose and fancy-free
traveller who is given the oracle's blessing to go where he
wants. He is also urged to see the great man. In other words,
the leader is being told to pay attention to the alternative
message of the traveller.

Finally, 58 sums up the feelings of the oracle about this
enigmatic, contrary figure: 'Delight. Make the offering and
benefit from the oracle.'

The Home-Coming

HEXAGRAMS 59–61
This brings us to what we would describe as the third section
of the *I Ching*. We term this 'The Return'.

In 59 we have the clearest oracle, speaking about the return of
the king to his ancestral temple, exactly as the *Shu Ching*
describes. To do so he has to recross the great river, retracing
his steps.

By Hexagram 60, the king is beginning the sacrifices and is
given a command concerning his style of kingship: restraint,
but benevolent restraint. He is being reined back by his oracle
from abuse of power.

In 61, we have a description of the offerings and then a
description of the king, newly blessed, returning to his freshly
conquered state, again crossing the great river.

The Final Warnings

Finally we come to the last three oracles. Here we move into one of the most intriguing sections of the text.

Hexagram 62 speaks of problems – not major ones, but problems all the same. It indicates that from now on the oracle will deal with minor issues, but as for power politics, it will have nothing to do with them. It is as if the oracle is beginning to disassociate itself from the consequences of conquest. Using the image of a bird on the wing, it suggests that such a creature should beware of constantly rising higher and higher. Eventually it will have to come down. Another coded warning to the powerful that if they forget themselves they will be humbled.

So we come to the last two hexagrams. Here the oracle speaks clearly and disturbingly. The two final hexagrams are titled 'Finished' (63) and 'Unfinished' (64). The titles alone give the sense of what the *I Ching* is trying to say. Just when you think all is completed, finished, summed up and dealt with, that is the point at which it all unravels.

Hexagram 63 says so quite explicitly: 'At the start, good fortune; at the end, chaos.'

Then 64, using the image of an inexperienced fox, puts the final dampener on any sense of triumph that the king might have felt. It speaks of a young fox who, when crossing the stream, gets his tail wet. The oracle seems to be saying that victory is all very well, but with such triumph comes sorrow and trouble. It is perhaps one of the most remarkable aspects of the whole *I Ching* that the final line of the final oracle of this epic of struggle, battles, conquest and power denies the whole venture. It says, 'Nothing is going well.'

The Epic as Personal and Public Story

Why does the *I Ching* end like this? Why would the shamans have ended with such a text? Our contention is that the *I Ching* is of such importance precisely because it deals with the whole panoply of human emotions, from struggle to triumph to struggle again. At the annual retelling of the conquest, through the dancing and the reciting of the oracles, the epic would have been acted out. But at each annual gathering, the problems of the day would have been as present in people's minds as they are for us now. In such a setting, a triumphant ending would have left people feeling that they were unequal to the heroics of their illustrious ancestors, that all problems should have disappeared and any difficulties they were experiencing were their own fault. The final text, the last oracle, says, 'No, trouble and chaos are as much part of life, if not more so, than triumph and conquest.' What makes the *I Ching* so powerful to this day is its recognition of the eternal nature of change, transformation and struggle. This is why, at the end of a heroic epic, it is doubt, it is the lone individual, it is dissent from power politics and it is recognition of the troubles of life which culminate the whole story.

As we said at the beginning, the *I Ching* has become a great spiritual text because it speaks to the human condition in whichever generation encounters it. That it can now be shown to be rooted in a historic event adds to its significance in the same way that the Exodus experience has been an inspiration for people's struggles, individual and collective, down the centuries. The epic of the *I Ching* is the epic of the changing nature of life, its ups and downs and its difficulties. What is so fascinating is the Voice that is to be heard within it, a Voice which finds an echo in the lives of all who use it. It is this Voice which helps lift the text from being just a chronicle to being a spiritual journey.

THE TEXT

The Oracles, Lines and Wings

Historically, there are three layers of text within the *I Ching*. The first layer is that of the oracles. These are traditionally called the 'judgements' and are the opening text which carries the title of the hexagram and the oracle text.

The second layer is that of the lines. These sets of six lines (seven in the case of the first two hexagrams) in each hexagram have short texts attached to them.

The third layer is that of the wings or commentaries. These are essentially essays on the *I Ching*, reputedly written by

Confucius *c.* fifth century BC, but actually dated some 200 or 300 years after him. In this translation we have not included the wings as such, but the Modern Commentary for each hexagram and each line draws upon classical commentaries such as the wings, as well as upon modern commentaries. In doing so, I have tried to give the sense of a sort of contemporary shamanic voice and sought to let the oracle speak in perhaps a somewhat less confusing way than it does in some of the texts.

The Oracles

The oldest layer of text, which we have termed 'oracle', consists of the 64 initial texts introducing each hexagram. These are traditionally called 'Judgements', but, following the work outlined above, we feel they are better named 'oracles', for this is what they are. These texts, as discussed above, are the original oracles associated with the revolt of the Chou against the Shang in the eleventh century BC and their subsequent conquest of the Shang empire. Dating from a remarkably short period of time, perhaps as little as a year, they represent the oracles which guided the Chou tribes to victory. As such, as already mentioned, they were probably recited annually at the celebration of the conquest at the Chou ancestral temple. They would have been collected in order to illustrate the progress of the conquest, but also to highlight the dangers of power and the troubles and woes that afflict even, or maybe especially, the successful.

We would assert that these original oracles formed the first text of the *I Ching* or, as it was known from its conception until around the fourth to third century BC, the *Chou I* – 'Changes of Chou'.

Trigrams and Hexagrams

What is impossible to tell is where the notion of affixing the oracles to the 64 hexagrams came from. The basis for the hexagrams is the eight trigrams:

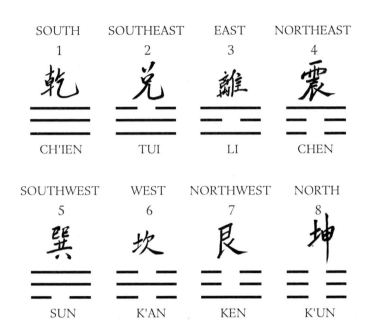

The eight trigrams.

These eight sets of three lines, either broken or continuous lines – the broken signifying yin and the continuous yang – are traditionally associated with the figure of Fu Hsi. He is a mythological figure, part human, part snake, who supposedly lived around 3000 BC and taught humanity the skills of agriculture. His discovery of the eight trigrams is recorded in 'The Great Commentary' which forms one of the major appendixes to the *I Ching* (see below).

> *When in ancient times Fu Hsi ruled all below Heaven, he looked up to observe the phenomena of the Heavens and gazed down to observe the contours of the Earth. He observed the markings of birds and beasts and how they adapted to their habitats. Some ideas he took from his own body, and went beyond this to take other ideas from other things. Thus he invented the eight trigrams in order to comprehend the virtues of spiritual beings and represent the conditions of all forms of creation. He knotted cords and made nets for hunting and fishing. This idea he probably adopted from the hexagram Li.*
> ADAPTED FROM THEODORE DE BARY (ED), *SOURCES OF CHINESE TRADITION* VOL.1, P 197, COLOMBIA UNIVERSITY PRESS, 1960.

Other legends associated with Fu Hsi say that he discovered the eight trigrams, along with the map of the heavenly constellation, upon the shell of a sacred turtle which emerged from the sea as he stood on the shore. As we have seen, the links between the hexagrams and the oracle tradition of using turtle shells for divination are fundamental to the actual history of the *I Ching*.

In all likelihood, the eight trigrams and their consequent combinations into the 64 hexagrams date from the time of the Chou themselves.

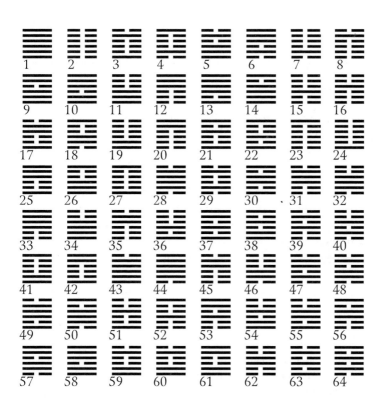

The 64 hexagrams.

There is no evidence for the eight trigrams being known in the Shang dynasty. They do not feature in the art of the period. Indeed, it appears likely that the trigrams emerged as a result of a distinct Chou dynasty change in divination methods. They are essentially a substitute for the oracle bones, with the three lines representing basic crack patterns on the bones or shells. The hexagrams have always been associated with divination plants, in particular yarrow sticks, and use of the yarrow sticks was only developed under the Chou.

Perhaps one can see in this shift something of the worries that the oracles in the *I Ching* spoke about. It would appear that the use of divination shells and bones gradually fell into disuse. Such methods came to be seen as cumbersome and rather old-fashioned, associated with both a discredited dynasty – the Shang – and with a rather primitive tribal past, based around the sacred mountain of Ch'i Shan. With the shift of the centre of the Chou dynasty to the former Shang lands, Ch'i Shan fell into provincial obscurity and does not even count today as one of the historic sacred mountains of China.

If this is the case – and certainly many scholars believe that the eight trigrams are a Chou invention based on yarrow sticks (see for example Fung Yu-lan's *A History of Chinese Philosophy*, Vol.1. pp.379–81, Princeton University Press, translated by Dirk Bodde, 1952) – then the oracles pre-date the hexagrams. Quite when and why they became combined is unclear. No mention is made of the hexagrams in other texts until, at the very earliest, the eighth century BC. The text in which the oracle is mentioned as having been consulted in that century is actually from the fourth century BC, but there are sufficient references from the sixth century BC onwards to conclude that the *I Ching* as we know it was definitely formed by then.

Our contention therefore is that the oracles were a distinct unit from the eleventh century BC.

The Lines

The second layer of the *I Ching* is the lines. These are the statements attached to each of the six lines of each hexagram. We believe that these are a combination of other oracle readings, proverbs, wisdom sayings and peasant insight. As such they reflect a similar variety of sources to those which form the sayings sections of each of the chapters of the *Tao Te Ching* (see *The Illustrated 'Tao Te Ching'* by Kwok, Palmer and Ramsay, Element Books, 1993, pp.10–13).

It is clear that some of the line statements have a historical root. For example, in Hexagram 11, line 5, and again in Hexagram 54, line 5, the name 'Emperor Yi' is found in association with his marrying off his younger sister. Emperor Yi was a Shang dynasty king, the father of Emperor Chou. While the reference makes some sense in 54, which is the oracle concerning not marrying the younger sister, it is unclear what connection it was thought to have with 11. The most likely explanation is that the basic 64 oracles, while supplying a foundational narrative of epic proportions, did not supply sufficient data for the emerging urban diviners who no longer resorted to oracle bones per se for all questions and requests for divination.

Quite why or how the lines were formed is unclear. That the material in them is ancient is beyond question, but whether they contain material which began life originally as sayings or recorded oracles during the Shang dynasty and then the early Chou dynasty or whether they arose only after the Chou conquest is impossible to say. Whatever their history, they were added to the oracles at a later date.

Because attention has tended to focus upon the lines rather than upon the oracles, the distinctive nature of the oracles has been largely overlooked. We would argue from both historical evidence and from the starker stylistic nature of the oracles, that they are an earlier strand than the lines. This would mean that the lines are from the earliest centuries of the Chou dynasty. Our feeling is that as the oracles were recited each year, and as people came to see them as more than just an historical story, so the expectation that they could be used for continued 'revelation' led to them accruing other oracle sayings and wisdom proverbs. The legendary history of the lines seems to bear this out. While King Wen is credited with inventing the oracle texts, it is a later figure, Duke Chou (or, according to some accounts, King Wu) who is named as the author of the lines. In other words, even legend recognizes that the oracle texts came first, with the lines second.

The Wings

The third layer of the *I Ching* is the so-called 'wings', commentaries such as 'The Great Commentary' from which we quoted earlier. These were composed much later. Legend ascribes them to Confucius (551 to 479 BC), though it is highly unlikely that he had anything to do with them. Most scholars now see them as being fourth or third century BC texts.

In this translation, we have only included the most ancient texts, namely the oracles and the lines. This is in line with our desire to return to the shamanistic roots of the text. This is highlighted by Jay Ramsay's poems, which accompany each hexagram. Drawing upon insights into the meaning and symbolism associated not just with each oracle, but also with the particular trigrams which make up each of the hexagrams, Jay has produced a modern shaman's oracle. In his poems he has sought to speak as a shaman oracle would speak and to cast some light not only upon the historical narrative, but also upon the perennial wisdom and our contemporary spiritual journey, which is the other side of the power of the *I Ching*.

It is to the shamans that we now want to turn.

FROM SHAMAN TO CLASSIC AND BEYOND

Shamanism can lay claim to being the oldest world religion. Originating at least 8,000 years ago in Siberia, it spread across the then existing land bridge between Siberia and Alaska, and thus down through North America. It is the basis for much of what we now know as Native American religion. In similar fashion, it spread down into China, Korea and across to Japan. Its traces here are to be found in much of contemporary Taoism and in aspects of Shinto in Japan. Its influence spread West along the migration routes of the Steppe peoples, reaching into northern Europe, where traces of it are to be found in Finland and Norway, and spreading South beyond China into South East Asia.

The heart of shamanism is its belief in two worlds: the material, physical world which we inhabit and experience, and the superior, spiritual world, which exists alongside this world and sometimes breaks through into it. The role and power of the shaman is her or his ability to communicate between these worlds. This is done through trance states and through being taken over by an animal spirit – in Siberia and much of northern China, the spirit of a bear.

Through such states, the shaman could ask questions of the spirit world concerning problems in the material world such as illness or disasters. The concern of shamanism is to help humanity live in accordance with the wishes and flow of the spiritual world. To be out of kilter with the spiritual world is to be in trouble. To be in the flow of the spiritual world is to go with the forces of life. This notion lies behind the later developments of Taoism, especially as expressed in the *Tao Te Ching*, where the goal of human existence is to be part of the Tao, the Way, that flows on and on for ever.

This is why oracles were so important. Before undertaking any great venture it was important to ascertain whether the ancestors and Heaven were on your side. At death, the ancestors became part of the spirit world and therefore were another channel through which requests and petitions could be addressed to the spirit world of Heaven. As we have seen, under the Shang dynasty, even the most mundane questions could be asked of the oracle.

For the petitioners of the Shang and Chou dynasties, the Voice which they heard speaking to them from the oracles, through the shamans, was a multi-faceted Voice. It was in part the Voice of the ancestors. It is not without significance that the annual re-enactment, through dance and recitation, of the conquest of the Shang by the Chou took place at the Chou ancestral temple. But there were other aspects to the Voice. There was the notion of some primal force which also spoke through the oracles and shamans. Some commentators have tried to make this primal source similar to the Western notion of God. I don't believe this is warranted by the texts. What seems to have been meant was a sense of there being a higher world, the spirit world, which overshadowed this world. The classic description of this is contained in the traditional Chinese triad of Heaven, Earth and humanity. Heaven created all, Earth nourished all and humanity's role was to balance all.

By the sixth century BC, this sense of an original primal force had been captured in the credal statement of the *Tao Te Ching*. Chapter 42 says:

The Tao
gives birth to the One:
The One
gives birth to the Two;
The Two
give birth to the Three –
The Three give birth to every living thing.

All things are held in yin, and carry yang:
And they are held together in the ch'i *of teeming energy.*
ILLUSTRATED 'TAO TE CHING', KWOK, PALMER AND RAMSAY,
ELEMENT BOOKS, 1994.

The Two referred to here is of course the yin and yang
combination, and *ch'i* is the original breath which every living
thing has. When this *ch'i* expires, then death follows.

At the time that the *I Ching* was being finalized in the seventh
to eighth century BC, concepts of Tao and yin and yang were
very basic. Indeed, there is no evidence that the earliest texts,
the oracle texts, would have known anything of yin and yang.
These two fundamental cosmic forces, the one – yin – dark,
watery, female; the other – yang – light, fiery, male, which
came to be so central to Chinese philosophy, were simply
unknown in the eleventh century BC. But the seeds of their
emergence, along with that of the Tao as the ultimate force
behind even the Origin, were there in the shamanistic
perceptions of a superior spirit world.

The Decline of the Shamans

Shamanism seems to have held a dominant position for many
thousands of years, until the emergence of large settled
communities. If hints in the most ancient records are to be
believed, women originally played the most senior role in
shamanism – namely, most shamans were women. However, in
line with changes which it is claimed were taking place world-
wide in the second millennium BC, men gradually took over
more and more power and ousted the women.

Under the Shang dynasty, shamanism as a political religious
structure reached its apogee. The shamans were officers of
immense importance within the Court and their power to
command monumental sacrifices and offerings was never

remotely equalled in the Chou dynasty. Furthermore, as discussed above, the power of the shaman began to be replaced by oracle or divination texts, accessible to people other than shamans – the *I Ching* being a classic example. With the emergence of written divination texts which claimed powers of revelation independent of a shaman, the days of the all-powerful shaman at Court were numbered.

Interestingly, the tag of being a shamanistic text in origin means that the *I Ching* – or *Chou I*, as it was then – did not receive serious attention for nearly 1,000 years. While Confucius in the sixth century BC is credited with holding it in high esteem and also with writing the wings (which, as already mentioned, he certainly did not), and the Confucian scholar Hsun Tzu (third century BC) mentions the book in passing, no other significant philosopher paid the *I Ching* the slightest attention until about 213 BC. In that year, the first true Emperor of what we consider China, the tyrant Ch'in Shi Huang Ti, ordered the destruction of all books, especially any history or philosophy texts. The reasons for this terrible action were that Ch'in Shi Huang Ti wished to eradicate all memory of any other way of life than that of the harsh, brutal military regime which he instituted. However, in the list of books which were exempted from burning were books on agriculture and books of divination, including the *Chou I*.

The Chou I *becomes the* I Ching

From the silence of writers and philosophers such as Lao Tzu, Mencius, Chuang Tzu and Lieh Tzu, we can assume that the *Chou I* was not seen as being of any particular philosophical or cosmological significance. Indeed, it is quite likely that it was seen as being rather primitive. Then, for reasons which are not clear, the *Chou I* becomes one of the Five Classic texts, hence its change of name, for the classics are called *Ching* – which simply means 'classic'. So the *Chou I* becomes the *I Ching*. Why? We really do not know. For some reason, perhaps associated with the assumed links to Confucius, the *Chou I* moves into the most prestigious collection of books in the whole of China. For the Five Classics were the core texts of all studies in China for over 2,000 years. Prior to the start of the Han dynasty in 207 BC, the Five Classics included a book called the *Yo Ching*, which the *I Ching* ousted and which has been lost to us. With the promotion to the big time league, the *I Ching* begins its quite remarkable ascent to the position of the paramount wisdom book of China.

While only Confucius, the philosopher Hsun Tzu and the historian of the *Shu Ching* had noted the *Chou I* in the nearly 1,000 years from its beginnings in the eleventh century BC, during the Han dynasty (207 BC–AD 220) hundreds of commentaries were written on the *I Ching*, 20 or more of which we still have today. The book's elevation to the Classics accounts for much of this, but at the same time, something was happening to people's perceptions of the book which was to mark its development for the next 1,900 years. As the mystique of the shamans wore off, the *I Ching* in turn began to develop a mystique. It began to be seen as the one book within which all knowledge could be found.

This reached quite extraordinary levels during the T'ang and Sung dynasties (T'ang – AD 618–906; Sung – AD 960–1126). For example, the AD eleventh-century philosopher Ch'eng I commented:

> *There is not a single thing that those who made the I did not conjoin, from the obscure and bright of heaven-and-earth to the minute subtleties of the various insects, grasses and trees.*
> QUOTED IN *SUNG DYNASTY USES OF THE 'I CHING'*, SMITH ET AL., PRINCETON UNIVERSITY PRESS, 1990.

The level to which wild speculation and fantasy concerning the meaning of the *I Ching* had reached led the great Sung dynasty philosopher Chu Hsi (AD 1130–1200) to produce what in effect was a standard edition of the *I Ching*. This massive work, distilling and dismissing much of the more speculative material of the previous thousand years, became the guiding light for serious study of the *I Ching* until the 1715 imperial edition.

But while it stilled some of the more spectacular notions at scholarly levels, the *I Ching* continued to be developed as a magical text or alchemical text by practitioners of folk religion. By the fifteenth century, it was included in official Taoist texts along with a swathe of commentaries.

In 1644 the last ethnically Chinese dynasty fell. The Ming dynasty, worn out by corruption, collapsed before the onslaught of the Mongolian forces and with the fall of Peking in 1644, the Ch'ing dynasty (1644–1911) came into existence. The demise of the Ming and the arrival of the 'barbarian' Ch'ing dynasty caused massive upheaval within China, not just at a social and political level, but on the intellectual level as well. It unleashed a wave of critical studies of the Classics, which prefigured much of what is now called historical and literary criticism. The *I Ching* did not escape this intellectual ferment. For example, Hu Wei, in the late seventeenth century, argued that the trigrams and hexagrams of the *I Ching* were a much later addition – claiming that they were in fact Taoist inventions and thus dated from only the first or second century AD.

The turmoil caused by such statements, as well as other critical studies of 'sacred' texts such as the *Shu Ching*, deeply disturbed the Ch'ing Emperors, who saw themselves as being guardians of traditional Chinese values – while their opponents saw them as barbarians! In the reign of K'ang-hsi (1662–1723) steps were taken to reassert orthodoxy and in particular to assert the right of the Ch'ing to rule. In 1715, drawing upon Chu Hsi's masterpiece of the twelfth century, but culling material and commentary from many other scholars from the Han dynasty onwards, K'ang-hsi issued what became the definitive edition of the *I Ching*, the imperial edition. Deeply conservative, deeply reactionary, it was also politically slanted to justify the foreign rule. It was this edition which the West first encountered and from which the somewhat incomprehensible translations and interpretations of translators such as Legge and Wilhelm came.

In working on this translation we have used a variety of Chinese editions of the text and have also referred where appropriate to the earliest extant copy of the *I Ching*, the second century BC text from Mawangdui in China, discovered in 1973.

Since the fall of the imperial family and the coming of first the Republic and then the Communist Party, much of the intellectual apparatus which supported the role and significance of the *I Ching* has been destroyed or faded away. Yet the *I Ching* goes from strength to strength. In China, it is the subject of enormous academic interest, much in the same way as acupuncture is. While much of the 'spiritual' significance is officially denied, its power and authority is acknowledged.

Likewise, in cultures that are radically different from that within which the *I Ching* has grown – namely the West – it has become one of the most widely accepted books of inspiration and divination available. The *I Ching*, whatever else it may have been, has now become a common spiritual classic of the world. So what is it about and how do you use it?

THE PHILOSOPHY OF THE *I CHING* AND HOW TO USE IT

The introduction of the *I Ching* to the West has been a story of considerable confusion. The best known translations, those of Legge and Wilhelm, are sincere attempts to present a text which both men found confusing to a Western audience which was suspicious of the material. Both men were Christians and saw in the text the Hand of God at work, in much the same way and given at much the same time (so they believed) as the Jews were being given the Torah, first five books of the Bible. Thus their translations adopt a form of 'religious' language which they used to make it sound like a serious religious text. The result is confusion.

This was compounded in Wilhelm's case by the fact that he worked with a displaced academic. Wilhelm did his translation in the 1920s when the whole imperial edifice had collapsed. Nevertheless, he produced a text which was imperial in the extreme, for he worked with a scholar, Lao Nai-hsuan, whose whole world had fallen apart with the coming of the Republic in 1911. It is clear that Lao would have been considered fairly conservative at the best of times. In the turmoil of the Republic, he was positively reactionary! This is reflected in the very conservative vision of the *I Ching* which he imparted to Wilhelm.

Since Wilhelm, the *I Ching* has passed into popular culture. While some good new translations have been undertaken (notably by John Blofeld and Alfred Douglas), most of the books currently on sale claiming to be on the *I Ching* are, let me be charitable, imaginative reworkings of the Legge or Wilhelm texts. And I am afraid that quite a lot of what is written about the *I Ching* does not bear too close a scrutiny!

This is a shame, because it has often obscured the real power of the *I Ching*. The *I Ching* is not a book of answers. It will not tell you what to do. If you approach it in that spirit, you will either have to delude yourself or be disappointed. What the *I Ching* offers is guidance.

What it does is to put a different perspective on issues – a perspective which can often radically challenge or alter the way you have thought about something. What the *I Ching* is, is a Third Voice. You may feel this Third Voice is the Voice of Nature, of the Tao, even of the Divine. What you call it is irrelevant to the actual functioning of the *I Ching*. For the *I Ching* offers you, from the storehouse of human experience, enlightened by the interplay between the material and spiritual worlds of the shamans, and the Voice of the oracle, a way of listening to a Greater Voice.

Let me try and illustrate the use of the *I Ching*. You are confronted by a problem or a choice. Perhaps it is whether to continue with a relationship or to take up the offer of a new job which requires upheaval. You have tried to look at these issues from as many perspectives as possible. You still cannot decide what to do. You are torn by conflicting loyalty claims or interests. You are unsure whether to risk a new adventure or stay with the security you have. What you need is guidance. In such situations the *I Ching* comes into its own. For you are in exactly the same sort of dilemma that King Wu was in – do I attack Shang or not? Do I cross the river or not? What the oracle, the *I Ching*, does is to present you with a set of texts which come at your problem from a radically different perspective. Through the interaction between your situation and the life situations which gave rise to the *I Ching*, you are confronted with a vision or a question which helps to clarify your mind.

If you turn to the *I Ching* expecting it to tell you what to do, whether to go on with the relationship or to take the new job, you will rarely receive a straight answer. Instead, you will be offered a view of the issues at stake, which will leave you still with the decision to make, but you will now have a clearer – or radically altered – perspective from which to make that decision. This is the power of the *I Ching*. It does not so much answer your questions as push you along. In the end, just like King Wu, you have to decide what to do. Having done it, you may find the oracle takes you to task later for going too far or for ignoring something central in your actions. In other words, you should develop a dialogue with the *I Ching*, not look to it to command you or control you.

For many Chinese, the *I Ching* is a book used every day. Not with the cumbersome yarrow sticks or coins, but simply by opening the book at random and letting your finger indicate an oracle or a line. This then becomes a sort of 'Thought for the Day' or, if there is a particular worry in mind, an inspiration for dealing with that issue. We would recommend this method to everyone, for it gets rid of some of the hocus-pocus in which people like to try and wrap the *I Ching*. For the sole dynamic underpining its working is chance.

In our lives we attempt, usually against the odds, to keep control; we try to reason things out, plan things, struggle to resolve problems through our intellect or skills. The *I Ching* stands against all that and exposes the limitations of such attempts to control the changes of the world. It asks us to abandon any attempt at control or reasoning, and instead to let go and flow with the flow of Nature, of the Tao, of God, of the spirit world – in other words, with that which is beyond us. By simply relying upon chance, we allow entrance to that which we cannot usually hear because we are too busy thinking or plotting or reasoning. This is the heart of the *I Ching*: the breaking in of another view, over which we have no control, of which we understand little, but which asks us questions and puts us in a position of listening. This is why we recommend just opening the book at random and allowing whatever your finger lights upon to enlighten you. Then, as outlined above, you are still left with your reasoning powers and your intellect, but you have allowed something beyond yourself to break in and to alter how and what you now think about.

The *I Ching* began life as an oracle. The purpose of asking questions of an oracle is to hear from beyond our world, beyond our experience. This is still what the *I Ching* can offer. It doesn't matter what faith you have, if any. The *I Ching* is not divine. It is not God or a god speaking. For some it may bring insights from the Divine or just from the natural forces of change which create the universe – it depends what you believe. But whatever you believe, it asks you to surrender yourself from attempting to work things out. It asks you to listen and to ponder afresh. It asks you to let a wider vision inform you. And it does so through the drama of the human saga of struggle, triumph, problems and defeat.

As stated above, we recommend the method employed by most Chinese, which is to simply open the book at random and allow the text to speak to you. However, there are three major systems which will be known to some and which many like to use. We shall give details of all three.

The Yarrow Stick System

In 'The Great Treatise', which is one of the wings of the *I Ching*, there is a description of how to consult it. The basic instruments are yarrow sticks, which are believed to have magical powers. In the imperial past, yarrow sticks grown on the tomb of Confucius at Qufu were considered the most auspicious.

'The Great Treatise' says the following:

> *[The stalks] are manipulated by threes and fives to determine [one] change; they are laid on opposite sides, and placed one up, one down, to make sure of their numbers; and the [three necessary] changes are gone through with in this way, till they form the figures pertaining to heaven or earth.*
>
> QUOTED FROM 'YI KING', TRANS. JAMES LEGGE, IN THE *CHINESE CLASSICS*, PP. 369–70, PARA. 61, 1871.

The yarrow stick method has largely fallen out of use amongst modern-day Chinese practitioners, but it has been made popular in the West through various translations. In ancient China, 50 sticks were used, which, through a highly complex system of chance, were divided and subdivided into groups which eventually gave a number which indicated whether you had a straight, yang line or a broken, yin line. Starting from the bottom of the hexagram, you built up the sequence through this method.

Today, if the yarrow sticks are used, they are limited to just 12. Six are marked as indicating yin lines and six as indicating yang lines. Calming the mind and offering the question or issue to be considered, you pull six of the sticks out. The first one out forms the bottom line of the hexagram and so on until you have constructed the hexagram *(see chart below)*. As no one line is highlighted, the entire hexagram is read.

TRIGRAMS UPPER LOWER	Ch'ien	Chen	K'an	Ken	K'un	Sun	Li	Tui
Ch'ien	1	34	5	26	11	9	14	43
Chen	25	51	3	27	24	42	21	17
K'an	6	40	29	4	7	59	64	47
Ken	33	62	39	52	15	53	56	31
K'un	12	16	8	23	2	20	35	45
Sun	44	32	48	18	46	57	50	28
Li	13	55	63	22	36	37	30	49
Tui	10	54	60	41	19	61	38	58

The Three Coin System

Another method often cited in translations is to use three coins. In pre-Revolutionary China (pre-1911) all coins were made to symbolize Heaven and Earth. The round shape of the coin stood for Heaven, while the square hole in the centre stood for Earth. This reflects the Temples of Heaven and of Earth in Peking. The Temple of Heaven is a series of round platforms one on top of each other. The Temple of Earth is a series of square platforms likewise constructed. One side of the coin was inscribed with the dynasty name and the Emperor's name and this counted as the yin side.

Wilhelm has a good description of how to use this system:

Three coins are taken up and thrown down together, and each throw gives a line. The inscribed side counts as yin, with the value of 2, and the reverse side counts as yang with the value of 3. From this the character of the line is derived. If all three coins are yang, the line is 9. If all three are yin, it is a 6. Two yin and one yang yield a 7 and two yang and a yin yield an 8.

THE '*I CHING*' OR *BOOK OF CHANGES*, TRANS. WILHELM, ENGLISH TRANS.
CARY F. BAYNES, ROUTLEDGE & KEGAN PAUL, 1951, P.724.

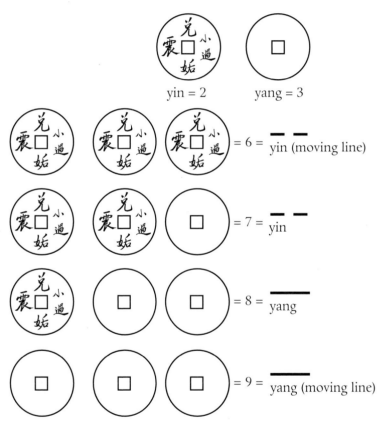

Three coin system.

Using this system, the enquirer arrives at a full hexagram, which can then be consulted. However, if any of the lines are either a 6 or a 9 – in other words, pure yin or pure yang – these are called moving lines, which means that they are lines of specific import for you and they can be changed. By changing them to their opposite – so a 6 becomes a 9 and vice-versa – a whole new hexagram is formed, which you can also consult. So, for example, Hexagram 49, which has a top line of 6 and a third line up of 9, becomes Hexagram 25 when these two are altered.

6 (moving line)
8
8
9 (moving line)
7
8

Hexagram 49   converts to   Hexagram 25

Moving lines.

The Pa Ch'ien system

The system which appears to be most common and popular amongst the Chinese themselves, and is certainly to be found in use at fortune-telling stalls in temple grounds where the *I Ching* is consulted, is the Eight Coin system, known as the Pa Ch'ien system.

For this, you need the eight trigrams set out in the order in which tradition says they were given to Fu Hsi, when he espied them on the back of the sacred turtle.

You also need eight coins, one of which is marked or indicated in some way as being different – for example, a blob of white paint. While it is considered most desirable to use old Chinese coins with their Heaven/Earth symbolism, any coins can be used.

Having calmed the mind and prepared the question, you then shake the eight coins together and then at random, lay them down, one by one, around the Fu Hsi chart, resting one against each of the trigrams. It is customary to start laying

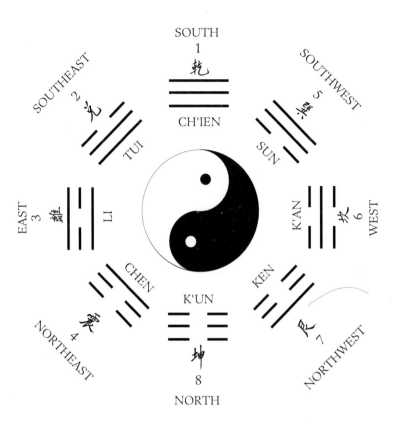

Fu Hsi chart.

them out from Ch'ien, the South trigram (please note, traditional Chinese maps always put the South at the top), but as chance is all important, this need not be adhered to too rigorously! Once the marked coin has appeared alongside one of the trigrams, you can stop, for this has given you the bottom three lines. Repeat the process to find the top three lines. This has given you the hexagram.

For example, in the first round, the marked coin has appeared beside Ken, the North West trigram.

NORTHWEST

7

KEN

On the second round, it appears beside Li, the East trigram.

EAST

3

LI

Using the chart for finding hexagrams from trigrams *(see page 42)*, you will find that Ken below and Li above gives you Hexagram 56, which is your reading. Then to find the specific line relevant to your enquiry, you take two unmarked coins away and then lay out the remaining six in an ascending line. Where the marked coin appears in the line is your specific line.

In this book, when you consult your hexagram and your line, you will have a variety of insights available. The oracle is the obvious starting-point, and this is complemented and enlightened by each poem of Jay's, which picks up on the essential aspects of the hexagram and of the oracle. You have in effect two shamanic oracles, one over 3,000 years old, the other of today. When you turn to the specific line you have been given, you will find the line text, also from the ancient Chinese past.

In Part Two, you have commentary on these ancient texts which may help you to apply the particular reading to your situation.

In Part Three we provide an exploration of the characters. This allows you to see what elements went into creating each specific character.

Combined, these should offer you the opportunity to hear the Voice which comes from beyond reason and beyond us. It should challenge and assist you. But remember, it still leaves you to make the decisions – for better or for worse!

INTRODUCTION

Jay Ramsay

The experience of writing these poems has been an adventure
of its own – an adventure that true to the essence of the book
has been profound, blood-fiery and life-changing ... and I
want to say something about that before moving on to offer
some reflections on it in terms of who we are and where we
are now. I want to do that because the *I Ching* is above all a
book that can be used. It is a manual for insight, for
transforming, initiating and guiding ourselves through a
wisdom grounded in lived and living experience of the
highest order.

The process goes back to when we'd finished working on the
Tao Te Ching in late 1991. Martin had the idea to do another
I Ching, to continue our collaboration, and at that stage asked
me for samples of poems for the opening hexagrams.

I had no idea where to start, but with pure intuition – going
into the argument and emphasis of each hexagram using his
Modern Commentary. I had no idea about form for the poems
either, since this wasn't translation, until I hit on the idea of a
six-line pattern corresponding to and mirroring the six lines of
each hexagram. It was all there was to grasp.

Subsequently, this first draft was abandoned – and the whole
project went on the back-burner for nearly two years. I only
mention the beginning because it is significant in retrospect:
we started 'up in the air' on a process of discovery and
uncovering that has increasingly taken us *down*, down into the
ground and into the bone. That began when we got back into
it in 1993, with the information about the oracle bones.
'Cracks in the bone' were what spoke most strongly to me and

I could feel that the nerve of the book was in there, alongside the figure of the shaman as he started to appear. We realized then that we were looking at archaeology – getting down through the layers to the origin, to the source where there was space and flint-sparks of light in the darkness.

We'd begun, but the real breakthrough didn't start to come until the snowy early part of 1994 when we spent a day and a half tracing the radicals or root meanings of each hexagram title through a Chinese dictionary, breaking the titles down as concepts into component images that were tangible and original. I could see space for the poems then, grounded in a real understanding and 'innerstanding' as opposed to airy speculation, and we agreed then that my main focus should be on them and on the ancient text, the original oracles themselves. Parallel, of course, to this was the historical discovery we were making as we went that only deepened the ground still further. Here, we realized, buried under a mound of metaphysics, was an actual story – a pattern and a sequence. Several other things were clear: the first was that the hexagrams are fundamentally shamanic interpretations given as a series of penetrating responses; the second was that for the leader or 'noble man' this was a process of guided initiation into kingship; and the third, quite simply, was that with guidance, with these oracles, *the project worked*.

Beginning the second draft then, I knew I wanted to represent three levels in what I was attempting: the first in 1100 BC at the time of the invasion itself; the second at a timeless level of essence and meaning; and the third as a way of echoing our own contemporary experience and situation. The discovery of the hidden story-line had a huge impact on me: I felt it had to be told and that I was in the position of the story-teller. At the same time I was debating inwardly the issue of clarity and accessibility on the one hand, and on the other the kind of cryptic brevity that these Zen-like cracks in the bone suggested. I wanted an oracle that could be understood, re-read, and used; and conversations by chance with various people who had been intrigued but bemused by the book reinforced this. At the same time I knew I was entering into a mystery – a mystery where real life experience had been generalized into a series of unerringly repeating situations – and that my task was to immerse myself in them.

This still left the issue of form for the poems on the page. What shape should they be? What length? Holding the thread of the narrative and working from the radicals we'd sketched along with our notes, what happened next was a process in reverse. Instead of building up each poem from notes, I found myself breaking it down from the draft, compressing it and deepening it until it began to feel right. The effect was rather like a series of Chinese boxes, or of moving inwards into the eye of a camera.

Martin was doing his digging and I was doing mine. The months passed.

What also began to surface then, uncannily, was a reflection of each hexagram I was working on synchronously in my own life. I would see, or sometimes be shown, each one's meaning – even to the extent of it being acted out in front of me. It was as if I'd entered into a kind of magnetic force field – and then I knew at least that somewhere the work was beginning to take hold. All I had to do was to keep my head down and my eyes open, and keep going.

I knew the drafts weren't the final thing. They were an education into the living fabric and depth of each hexagram – and with the help of friends, notably Carole Bruce and Lindsay Clarke, I was following the book's own advice to me to the letter. Be aware of the details, it said (no.62), beware of premature flight: be fluid (no.17) and then in the end be purely receptive (no.2), and it will all come together (no.8). A stray line in addition, describing a 'lower yellow garment', also advised discretion, or so I heard it. Meanwhile it loomed, like the mountain itself, shrouded in impenetrable silence. I asked for help and finally, thanks to Annie Wilson, guidance on rewriting them came.

What actually happened in the final draft came from a mixture of inspiration and the sheer build-up of energy around the work itself. I abandoned the idea of cryptic brevity and abandoned linearity in the individual poems. The three levels of time came together in an impasto and the poems suggested being read on all these levels at once. I found them being pitched into a timeless past that is also a timeless present – and I have tried in each case to give their meaning in contemporary form, drawing on my own experience, and my experience of them as states of mind and feeling. I have titled each of them accordingly, often with direct reference to the radicals (see Part Three), as well as cross-referencing and echoing off the main titles we have given each hexagram.

I have also been keen to draw on the theme of characterization that is part of every story, especially an epic, so there are 'The Young Son' (16), 'The Leader' (19), 'The One Who Stays' (25) and 'Shaman Woman' (37), among others, as well as 'The King' (55) and his foil 'The Traveller' (56), named after the famous Taoist poet Li Po, and also suggested by W. H. Davies and Alan Jackson. All of these characters are contemporary too, as I've indicated in no.52, which refers to J. Krishnamurti, and they are all states of being we can embody, as I'll be going on to explore.

The poems themselves came finally as variations on a broken sonnet form, as one breath, to be read in one go, and taken together they are a structure for the *I Ching* as I see it, spanning past and future, and anchored between the first two and the last two hexagrams, following the evocation of the tortoise in the prelude as living shell, substance and symbol. They are one interpretation among many possible others – and my hope is only that they can be of service to you in stimulating and catalyzing your own, written or lived.

In a book where so much is tenuous and uncertain, I am certain only of one thing: that the best way to understand these hexagrams is to live them, taking them as texts for your own experience. They are inexhaustible, as I realized working on them: they present themselves again and again. The *I Ching* is like a book of sand in this sense, or a series of slates that are constantly erased. So in addition to opening the book at random, as Martin has said, I want to suggest you take each hexagram as a meditation – or even as a visualization, to fill out with your own seeing and your own journey. You might like to think of when you've experienced a particular hexagram and what it describes, of where you were and what was happening to you and around you at the time. You may in turn like to add the simple exercise of allowing an image or picture to emerge from that experience and see what it might be trying to show you or say to you. This is one way we can use this extraordinary book now in a new way and my own experience is that it repays all our efforts. It isn't a book to be taken lightly, either, as so many commentators have pointed out: it is more like honouring a powerful and strange friendship – the more we put in, the more it yields. The *I Ching* is in every sense a book that lives in knowing it and it is worth studying the hexagrams independently of asking actual questions for this purpose.

There are two vital things to really understand about it as a book. The first is that everything you can take literally must also be taken metaphorically: it is in this way that its meaning expands and resonates across time, beyond the time that it actually happened. Story becomes allegory. So in no.9, for instance, the petty ones are both the fractious elements among the Chou tribes and the difficult elements in ourselves that won't fit into a higher undertaking, parts of our shadow, if you like, or even, in a concrete situation, things we have left out of our luggage in last-minute packing. The point of course in each case, with each reading, is to see where the significance lies – and it will usually point to something we may be aware of but are not giving enough emphasis to. So in this case, with no.9, it trips us up. We're not ready to move as we think we should be moving, or want to move, and so we're restrained. The book's strength lies in endless details of this kind, which is why the line readings are also important. What sparks or lights up for us could come from anywhere in its fruitful and fertile maze.

The second thing to understand about the book is that it is a life journey. This is where its sequence and the story it tells are so significant and profound. The *I Ching* offers us thresholds, oracle by oracle, from the mystery of origin and the grounding of spiritual energy in the body (Hexagrams 1 and 2, as a consequence), through birth, adolescence, the need for patience, the issue of disagreement and on, through its whole rich panoply as it unfolds ... and here again I would recommend following through the hexagrams and seeing what these thresholds mean to you, having grasped them as chapters in the story that they are. They describe all the main situations we are likely to be confronted by, both ordinary and esoteric, that one journey – the original tribal journey – created, so that even as we grow in time, and have grown, the thresholds and the things we need to learn that they represent remain the same, as we come to them again, as they come back round on the spiral. We still need to learn to look with feeling and compassion (no.20), we still need to learn to let go and offer up (nos. 57 and 50) ... and so it goes on, and in this sense, 3,000 years is nothing – life is still the journey it always was, if we could only understand it. And this is what the *I Ching* offers us as a structure of self-development – a structure that, to my mind, taken as a sequence, becomes increasingly complex, refined and astute. In every way, the challenge of it grows.

Within this, it is important too to say something about the function of the paradox that you will find in the frequent 'pairing' of the hexagrams. Paradox is the central dynamic of the book and the *I Ching* – true to the original spirit of yang and yin – proceeds through it. Paradox has two main functions here: the first is to subvert the idea of orderly progression, along with our ideas of how things will and should be; and the second is to undercut our more superficial ideas of good and bad, where those ideas are based more egoically than spiritually. Both of these areas relate to what we *need* rather than what we want; to what is true, as opposed to what is comfortable and convenient. The *I Ching* has a way of saying 'this is actually how it is', and this is where an understanding of process in relationship to it is so useful. We are in a process and the process changes. This is how it is at the moment and it will change. This introduces a third point: the *I Ching* is saying not only do things change, however good or bad they are, but they change because the picture or situation can never be taken only one way. A paradox means that: to take something both ways and not just one way. So, for example, in no.33, explicitly, we have the theme of disconnection explored negatively in terms of avoidance and denial, and positively in terms of conscious withdrawal and retreat. Taking this further, you could say that both are the shadow of each other: retreat is the positive shadow of avoidance, and avoidance or suppression is the negative shadow of retreat. You have to see it both ways, that is the point of it. You cannot get a whole or deep picture for a situation otherwise.

In terms of the sequence, you can see how this is rooted in the actual story with its progressions and reversals, its hold-ups and breakthroughs – true to life because drawn from life itself. Have a look, for instance, at no.11 and no.12 here. Later on, too, at a critical point, the figure of the king that the 'noble man' has become is undercut by the appearance of the traveller with his very different set of values. Again, the traveller is the shadow of the king here: he is all that the king is not, he is all that the king has left out. It is a turning-point in the whole story too, as the hexagrams that follow exemplify. The traveller raises the question of identity by being who he is, which leads to the theme of letting go, which in turn leads to the possibility of joy. So paradox is finally progression, too – real progress in the deeper scheme of things – and to have a mind attuned to paradox in this sense is to be open and responsive as opposed to being closed and coercive – an attitude that is essential to the Way or Tao it specifically becomes in the *Tao Te Ching*, in the figure of the sage.

Here in the *I Ching*, it is raw wisdom that is open like the air and the sky, like the Father without the Son, fathomless and inscrutable as the first hexagram suggests, in the origin behind The Origin, as a background that goes on and on like space into the velvet depth of night, at the time when the new day for the Chinese traditionally begins, long before the dawn. How it is, and why life is like this, is a secret the *I Ching* keeps. We can't explain it. But life requires paradox, so that we can see and keep seeing more deeply into it.

We can understand this in terms of ourselves too, if we humanize it as its story invites us to. We are all made up of different parts and personalities, or subpersonalities as they have been referred to. We all have something that is royal or capable of royalty in the true sense in us, and we all have – however atrophied it might be – the capacity to be intuitive and shamanic. As men and women, as Shakespeare knew, we are all king and traveller, wife, *puella* and shamaness or shaman woman. We are lost in crowds, and we are individual and alone. Parts of us are advanced and mature, parts of us can be correspondingly undeveloped and immature. We contain these parts and these contradictions; they are grist to the mill of our journey, and proof of why, as souls and psyches, we are still alive and unfinished. In this sense, too, every hexagram is a character or person in the personal situation in which we express and embody it. We are patient or impatient, modest or arrogant and pretentious. So we are the paradox, too. We are the journey and its evolution.

We can understand this also in what the book has to say about relationship – a theme I have tried to draw out along with the characters, particularly in the second and third sections (after no.31) because it is so much a part of our preoccupation these days. In the evocation of nos.38 and 39 and what they suggest, in the meeting of the king with the shamaness in no.44, in the sacrifice in no.50 and with 'The Marrying Maiden' (as Wilhelm had it) in no.54, there is a powerful subtext around what is appropriate and what is inappropriate, what literally works and what doesn't work – along with, I feel, a suggestion that we need to be whole or at home in ourselves to be in a process of relating. This is further emphasized by the book's constant reference to centring and the centre, being in our centre and our individual truth, and in that being in touch with our 'original purpose' that we can understand as the essence of our journey. And as we find it, and lose it, and find it again, the *I Ching* keeps returning to it in the Return the story itself becomes after no.60 and through no.61.

This is certainly taking these issues of wholeness, dependence and independence in a modern context, but a deep reading of the book does nothing to persuade us against doing this. On the contrary: our relationships may have changed outwardly, socially and culturally, but in essence they are the same – and for us now, the challenge of being in a relationship as a path of feeling and a mystery as opposed to controlling it through expectation, manipulation and imposed security is here for the taking, if we are ever to really know what love is and what it requires.

Love and life, beyond power and conquest; politics, spirituality, and the essence that goes beyond both, this is the note the *I Ching* reaches towards, specifically in no.62 ('The Small Things', as we've called it), and it is a prophetic note, too, that its ending strikes – detached as it is in the eyes of the shaman who has the first word and the last – and as passionately engaged, in a different way, in the recognition of what goes beyond him – or you and I. As a yoga of centrality, as a series of ongoing meditations on the centre and what is real and unreal, and as a constant evocation of what is permanent, within change, the *I Ching* finally transcends its own sequence as the cycle ends – only to begin, in the dawn light, again.

And while we still have time, may we hear it speak...

How to Use This Book

The *I Ching* is an organic book. It has grown and developed, indeed, in line with its name, changed, over 3,000 years of history. As a result, the text has layers of different meanings and uses. This is reflected in the various parts of this book and we have designed it in such a way as to enable you to use as many as possible. In a sense, this is a work book.

Part One contains the first layer, which is the original ancient Chinese. As our introductions have pointed out, the core of this is the oracle text, followed by the text on each of the lines. This, along with Jay's contemporary poems on the theme of each hexagram, is what forms Part One of the work book – titled the *I Ching*. Through these ancient texts you can hear the shaman. Because these texts have continued to speak directly to people down the centuries and now increasingly across cultures, we have left them as they were given: stark, uncompromising and often enigmatic. Through each of Jay's poems it is possible to begin to get under the skin of these insights. But to help you further there are two other major sections provided in the book.

In Part Two, we have provided a Modern Commentary, drawing upon classical commentaries from the fifth century AD onwards and in particular Chinese commentaries of today. These commentaries are designed to help open up the often cryptic texts in the ancient Chinese. For most Chinese, not just in our day but in earlier centuries, the ancient Chinese text was obscure or difficult to follow. For over 2,000 years the *I Ching* has had commentaries available with it to aid comprehension and use. This is what we offer in Part Two, the Modern Commentaries.

In Part Three, the Radicals, we offer something very unusual. This part takes apart the Chinese characters which are the title character of each hexagram. By doing so, we examine why these characters were chosen and what they, often quite literally, portray. Each character is made up of other characters based around one dominant character which is called the radical for the character. By looking at what characters were combined to create a new character, we can get inside the deeper meaning of the character.

This part of the work book offers a reflection on both the development of Chinese and on the ways in which certain core ideas, beliefs and visions have become trapped like flies in amber, inside the final characters as they have emerged down the millennia. The radicals are particularly relevant to Jay's poems because it was often through exploration of these that he found the key which opened each hexagram to him.

Finally, we offer an exercise, Cracking the Bone. This is intended to show how the oracle bones worked and how written Chinese emerged from this ancient art of divination.

In using the book we suggest that you turn first of all to the ancient Chinese – Part One. Let it speak to you to the extent that it can and use Jay's poems as a meditation on the inner meaning of the hexagram.

Then we suggest turning to Part Two for the insights which 1,500 years of commentary on these very complex texts has provided.

Finally, we suggest using Part Three, the Radicals, to return you to a more contemplative approach to the *I Ching*.

It does involve moving around the book. But then the *I Ching* is no ordinary text, nor this an ordinary edition of it. By using the layers inherent within this exceptionally ancient text, you can reach back in time to the shamans of the mountain and forward to your own life. We hope you will.

Prelude: The Bone Speaks

I am tortoise –
The earth was planted on my back;
I am Black Warrior, massa confusa,
Guardian of graves, North and the winter,
They have raised monuments on me! I am essential.
I came out of the River with all the stars on my shell.

I am the table that does not break,
I am the stone that does not roll.
Can you look into my eyes now?
What are you seeing?

They slaughter me –
They slip a knife under my soft underbelly
As my feet splay, stretched to the four corners,
And my eyes close, life after life as they hold my head –
I have done this so many times before.

My substance is sacrifice
So I become permeable, membrane, I become veil
For their invisible world to shimmer through
As they upend me like a scoured womb...

They take me, and they drill holes in my sides;
They heat rods, beside me, in the crackling fire
And then they hold them to the holes, one by one,
As they scorch until I begin to crack
Fissure – and blister – and split

– and as I crack, I begin to speak –

Bone, I speak

Mountain, river, field and song

Man, kingdom, traveller and Way

In the shapes they draw out with their eyes,
Poring over me like a spread scroll
As they keen to the question in the mountain air.

Now listen:
I am bone, I am the beginning of written tongue,
In the cracked pictograms of Eye, I am –
I am bare tooth, bear skin and trepanned skull –
I am Creation that came before the Word, and I am now –

In my cave are all your imaginings.

1

I CHING

৷ ৷ ৷ ৷ ৷ ৷ ৷ ৷ ৷

1

Perfect Day, One

CREATOR: sun-blaze, greater than bone,
First father of the world in the dark before the dawn
As the hour of the new day breaks on the mountain –
First cause and first alignment: yours to make now –
And with the sun in your forehead.

                                            Source.

Heaven comes first, remember.

And yes, it says, perfect to the power of ten,
As the sun stretches over the sky –
And the whole earth rises to meet it:
This light in you is the fruit of the original tree,
Golden apple,

                        taste it.

Ch'ien: *this is the beginning of your journey.*

1

THE ORIGIN

Ch'ien

乾

Original offering, favourable oracle.

FIRST NINE

Diving dragon, do not use.

SECOND NINE

See the dragon visible in the field. Auspicious to see a great man.

THIRD NINE

The nobleman is active throughout the day. In the evening, cautious. Oppressive. No problem.

FOURTH NINE

Leaping up from the waters. No problem.

FIFTH NINE

The dragon flies in the heavens. Auspicious to see a great man.

UPPER NINE

Arrogant dragon needs repentance.

ALL NINE

A group of dragons are seen without heads. Good fortune.

Ground, Earth, Yin

CENTRING, earth, middle of –

Middle of you –

Where my finger points into your navel...
Into the belly of the earth, breathe down,
Breathe down the sun into the earth's depth of you,
And then move.

And how do you move? You see a horse up the lane,
Clopping in the rhythm of her nodding head and hooves,
And we say, like her, look! Receive her –
She is your strength, the whole earth moves with her

She is your mother.

She is the sun in the light of the rising moon.

Be like her.

2

THE RECEPTIVE

K'un

Original offering, favourable divination, like a sound mare. The noble man has to move. Takes initiative, fails. Obtains and finds the right one. Auspicious to have friends in the South West and to lose friends in the North East. Right oracle brings good fortune.

FIRST SIX

Walking on fresh frost, worse is to come.

SECOND SIX

Square, straight, great. No effort, all is well.

THIRD SIX

Virtue is hidden and sustained within. The oracle says some will serve the king and this is incomplete but has an end.

FOURTH SIX

A sack tied up. No blame nor praise.

FIFTH SIX

Imperial yellow undergarments. Excellent fortune.

UPPER SIX

Dragons battle in the wilderness. Their blood flows purple and yellow.

ALL SIX

Auspicious, for the oracle gives a good forecast.

Spring Aching Birth

The light is clear above your head
But don't be lulled, fooled –
You know the seed has to struggle in the dark

                                  to break through

Green, in all its gentle tip-and-bud unfurling...

Birth. Birth aches. And it's the same in you,
Breaking the surface to stand in your truth –

Wild birth. Anything could happen now,
The wind swings around you out of your womb of earth

It's a new air you are breathing, like wine
And you need your own kind with you.

3

BIRTH PANGS

Chun

Original offering. Favourable. Do not start something lightly. Advantageous to have hereditary leaders.

FIRST NINE

Difficulty moving ahead. Helpful to be settled. Useful to set up an hereditary ruler.

SECOND SIX

As if distressed and turned back. Horses of the chariot are likely to go back. Not an attacker. He wants her to be his wife. The woman is resolute and refuses. Ten years and she has children.

THIRD SIX

Hunting the deer without the forester. He finds himself in the midst of the forest. The nobleman is subtle. Not likely to advance. It will be a mistake to go ahead.

FOURTH SIX

The horses of the chariot are as if in retreat. Assistance is sought of the one who wishes to marry. To go forward is good. Highly likely to be auspicious.

FIFTH NINE

Difficult to bestow what is expected. In small things, the oracle is favourable. In big things, it is disastrous.

UPPER SIX

The horses of the chariot retreat. Tears like blood, flow.

Raising the Roof

You've asked me once and you've asked me again,
And I'm telling you: there's grass on your roof,
And your house is full of jumping adolescents,
Piglets! And that's you.

What am I saying? You aren't listening,
You're full of your own noise, greenhorn,
You think you know it all already anyway!
And you don't, you can't – you're not ready to.

And so what I'm showing you in my silence
Is a mirror to reflect in. Cool it, will you!

4

THE ADOLESCENT

Meng

The adolescent and success. It is not I who seeks out the youthful and the ignorant. It is they who seek me. A first divination reading is given, but when they ask for a second and then a third reading they abuse my friendship. Such rudeness does not deserve an answer. Report this favourable oracle.

FIRST SIX

To channel the inexperienced enthusiasm of the young, it makes sense to use punishment to help them to mature. It is important to be freed from constraints, though trying to leave can bring disappointment.

SECOND NINE

Take care of the young and you will have good fortune. To raise a family with a good woman and have sons to come after you is good fortune.

THIRD SIX

Do not marry this woman. See the golden husband without a body. There is nothing to be gained from such a person.

FOURTH SIX

To dwell in the midst of ignorance will only lead to regret.

FIFTH SIX

The innocent adolescent brings good fortune.

UPPER NINE

Attack the adolescent. Not good to be robbers, favourable for defending against robbers.

Rain, Again Rain

Patience, like the rain
– the heat gone out of the ground –
Waiting to fall,
And knowing it will
Rain, the rain whispering down...

Close your eyes and feel it. It takes time.
Hear its sound and feel its rhythm, breathing.
And then see it in everything, through your eyes...

You cannot force it, as hard as you try. Be wise to it.

And I see rain over the Great River
Grey on yellow, lighting your way to cross it:

And patience is the river, in the river's time...

5

PATIENCE

Hsu

There will be conquest and success if you make the right offering. The oracle foretells good fortune. It is favourable for crossing the great river.

FIRST NINE

Wait out at the rural shrine. You will do well to persevere, especially as the omens are good.

SECOND NINE

He is waiting on the sand. The ordinary people like to gossip but in the end there is good fortune.

THIRD NINE

He is waiting in the mud and so robbers arrive.

FOURTH SIX

He is waiting in a bloody place. He must escape from this hole.

FIFTH NINE

He is waiting amidst the wine and food. The oracle says good fortune.

UPPER SIX

He goes underground. There are three uninvited guests. Be generous to them and good fortune will come to you in the end.

Out in the Open

Teething aches in a baby's mouth,
Raised voices everywhere. You can hear them
Even as we speak – it's all out in the open,
And it's inevitable at this stage of things:
Everyone is certain they're right –
One sees it like this, another like that –
And it has to burn out and blow over...

The purpose evokes it. The pressure.
Unity, togetherness, comes later: and so for now
You are stranded this side of the river
This side of the Promised Dream and the future:
And while you are

Come back to your first steps

                every step of the way.

6

DISAGREEMENT

Sung

Despite difficulties he is confident. Be cautious. What looks to be going well can end in misfortune. It is favourable to see the great man, but it is not favourable to cross the great river.

FIRST SIX

Do not prolong things. There will always be gossip but there will be good fortune at the end.

SECOND NINE

There is no way of winning the argument. Retreat home swiftly to the town of 300 households. To do so is not a mistake.

THIRD SIX

Eat what is old. The oracle says there is danger but good fortune will come at the end. For anyone employed in the service of the king, such work is without end and it is impossible to settle all disagreements.

FOURTH NINE

Unable to maintain the dispute, it is better to retire and study how fate works. Things get worse. There is an oracle. This will bring good fortune.

FIFTH NINE

By pursuing the case, there will come immense good fortune.

UPPER NINE

The leather belt of authority may be given to you, but it can also be taken away again three times before even the morning is out.

Crowds and Power

Crowds of people, see? Wearing caps: an army,
Or, like an audience, they need a performer –
They need one thing to centre round: a leader
Like thoughts, or they can't go anywhere...

They are waiting, it is waiting: for you.
You need one thing to centre them as you do yourself,
If you can see beyond yourself, too,

To the sun, to what is around your head.

Drive a stake into the ground, and see:
Here is the centre that the circle needs
To be its circumference

                    embracing...

And he is everywhere among them, and then
It gathers to its crest like a shining, standing wave!

7

THE ARMY

Shih

The oracle says, wise leaders, good, no misfortune.

FIRST SIX

The army tries to operate according to the pitchpipes and this is useless and brings disaster.

SECOND NINE

To be the commander at the centre is to have good fortune. There are no mistakes and so the king honours the commander three times.

THIRD SIX

The army's leader is a dead loss and this brings disaster.

FOURTH SIX

The army retreats and makes no mistakes.

FIFTH SIX

There is plenty to hunt in the field. The thing to do is to profit by catching them. Make no mistake. The eldest son is commander of the army while the youngest son is useless. The oracle says ill fortune.

UPPER SIX

The mighty prince is the commander. He establishes kingdoms and enhances the great families but does not draw upon lesser men.

Seven Rising

Seven, the magic seven! It couldn't be better.
Seven rising, in the blue-gold air...
You can believe it now: this is the circle.
Everything comes together there –
And the key is this: that you come together,
And enter the One Body that you are.

Nothing is more powerful. You can see it
In a silence running between all of your eyes
So you don't even need words to say it: you know,
And those who can't are barred out, by themselves,
As if by an invisible wall, with nothing.

And in them, you can see what you were before.

8

UNITY

Pi

The signs are good and the oracle is excellent. There are no bad signs. Do not delay but follow now, for this is right. The one who tarries will have bad luck.

FIRST SIX

Those captured make good comrades, make no mistake. There will be enough cups to overflow with loot. This will end and there will be problems which are auspicious.

SECOND SIX

Unity comes from within. The oracle says good fortune.

THIRD SIX

Uniting with villains.

FOURTH SIX

Unite with others outside your own circle. The oracle says good fortune.

FIFTH NINE

A wonderful unity. The king uses mounted beaters on only three sides, allowing the swiftest animals to escape on the fourth side. People from the cities don't understand this. Good fortune.

UPPER SIX

When there is no one to lead the army, bad luck arises.

The Petty Ones

Small, mean, petty: close to home, it says –
And it's them, the misfits, the won't fits, rebelling,
And in you ... even as the dark clouds gather
And stop overhead, filling the sky –
From the blessing place, promising rain and deliverance.
But see it this way: they are a gift, they temper you
You've got to be wholly ready before you can move –
Even as a stray drop lands on your forehead

– restraint, to your wings.

Be awake to it.

9

RESTRAIN THE LESSER

Hsiao Ch'u

Restrain the less important from offering the sacrifice. Heavy clouds come from the West, but there is no rain.

FIRST NINE

Return to the right way. Why should this be seen as wrong? Good fortune comes.

SECOND NINE

Good fortune comes after he has been lured back.

THIRD NINE

The carriage stops because of a fault in the wheel spokes. The husband and wife avert their eyes.

FOURTH SIX

There is a captive and the risk of bloodshed. Move cautiously and there will be no mistake.

FIFTH NINE

The prisoners are bound together. When material assistance is needed, rely upon the neighbours.

UPPER NINE

Everything fails when the rains fail, but life continues. The woman who asks the oracle is in danger. The moon is almost full and if the nobleman attacks there will be a disaster.

From the Dead

When we bring back a body from the dead – take care
When we handle his blue-grey dreaming flesh
As his eyes flicker ('He's back – be quiet, still!')
Or when we say you're treading on a tiger's tail,
You're walking on a razor's edge –
You think it's simply the ground and it isn't – mind out
And it's the same power you have to understand.

And in plain speech, it means this:
What you are about to do is dangerous.
And you must learn to walk, stalk, talk that way.

Now, say it.

10

WALKING CAUTIOUSLY

Li

Walking cautiously on the tiger's tail, the man is not bitten. This is auspicious.

FIRST NINE

Just walking forward carefully ensures that nothing goes wrong.

SECOND NINE

Walk the way with ease. The oracle says it is good for the prisoner.

THIRD SIX

The one-eyed man can see and the lame can walk. But anyone treading on the tiger's tail will be bitten and have bad luck. The army officer acts like a great commander.

FOURTH NINE

He treads upon the tiger's tail. Be careful! All can end well.

FIFTH NINE

Stepping out confidently, the oracle says troubles ahead.

UPPER NINE

Look at where you are going and study the signs. When all comes together, marvellous good fortune awaits.

The Water Carrier

The breeze blows from T'ai Chi – in the mountain,
Ch'ien and K'un are together in you,
Sun and moon – man and woman,
She is in you and you are in her
Your beginning is with you again –
The blessing of the air is like a globe of pearl between you,

And along the dusty road, as the story has it,
A man comes into your village carrying water
As he greets you silently, his blue eyes shining,
With the sky wrapped like a cloak around him, behind him,

As he hands it to you.

11

BENEVOLENCE

T'ai

Benevolently, the lesser ones leave and the great come. The offering is good.

FIRST NINE

Pulling up the grass brings other plants with it. Press on with the attack and good fortune will come.

SECOND NINE

Remain with the uncultivated. It is helpful to cross the river without using a boat. Do not ignore your friends or they will disappear. Do the right thing by taking the middle path.

THIRD NINE

Peace cannot exist without destruction. It is impossible to go forward without returning. The oracle talks of difficulties and there is no mistake. Do not worry. Virtue is rewarded and happiness arises.

FOURTH SIX

Constantly coming and going. Not well off but always dependent on his neighbours. Yet he is always confident and seizes what he wants.

FIFTH SIX

The Emperor Yi arranges the marriage of his younger sister and this joyful act brings great blessing.

UPPER SIX

The city walls fall into the moat. The army is useless. He tells his own people of their fate and the oracle is inauspicious.

Nil by Mouth

No mouth, closed: I will not speak
No mountain, no pearl, no unbroken sky
No blessing, no lovers and the water is dammed
Somewhere in an invisible pipe...

You're called to a halt and you can't see why.
Only, what is it about the beginning
The origin you still have to suffer
So it becomes as strong in you as stone?

I ask you silently with a silent gaze –
There's nothing more we can say. This is the mystery.
And you'll just have to lie, and wait.

12

BLOCKED

P'i

There are rebels. The noble man is unable to do anything. The oracle says, the great leave and the lesser ones come.

FIRST SIX

Pull up long grass and other grasses will come up with it. The oracle says good fortune for those who make the offering.

SECOND SIX

Meat offering. The lesser types have good fortune but the great man stops the bad offering.

THIRD SIX

He carries his shameful offering.

FOURTH NINE

It is wise to follow the fate which is given. Divide the farm properly and the bird of happiness will come.

FIFTH NINE

The great man is calm and rested, even though he is experiencing real difficulties. This is good. He runs and hides as if he were concealed in a thick mulberry bush.

UPPER NINE

To begin with difficult, but now the difficulty has been overthrown and the result is good.

Mass Openness

And then it reverses, it changes again:
The oracle says openness, talking, sharing together
Man, men, people – *and another way comes: friends,*
Companions when you are together

And as you look beyond where you are,
We see you gather, we see you taking turns openly,
And then all you have in you can forge your connection
And it needs you to be with Heaven now,

to be at your best,

No less, and then you can cross the river –

On a new spring day, with all its freshness behind you:
You can bring the whole thing into another dimension.

13

ALLIES

T'ung Jen

Allies will be found in the frontier lands. The offering is favourable to a crossing of the great river. The nobleman has a favourable oracle.

FIRST NINE

Allies come to the door. There is nothing wrong in this.

SECOND SIX

Allies sought within the family will bring trouble.

THIRD NINE

The allies hid in the wild, armed with weapons. They go to the hills but there is no uprising for three years.

FOURTH NINE

Standing on the walls of the city he cannot be overcome. This augers well.

FIFTH NINE

The allies start by crying and weeping but later laugh out loud. The great armies come together.

UPPER NINE

Allies are gathered at the rural altar. There is nothing wrong with this.

A Great Many Have

Heaven opens its hands:
Blue sky, harvest gold air and ripeness,
Gathered sheaves, richness, readiness now –

And it is the heaven in you that ushers it,
In the warm golden flow in your heart –
The heaven

that is stronger than fire

And lighter, gentler, generously tender...
And it is for all of you now: don't withhold it,
Give as you've been given it, and give freely,
Without expecting any of it back –
In it,

and under it,

you have everything you need
As its gladness spawns and multiplies

as it spreads like a glow between you...

And it's the bread you have

and the manna

and the zest for your journey.

14

ABUNDANCE

Ta Yu

Great offering.

FIRST NINE

Beware of having any dealings with difficult or dangerous people or places. Understand this properly and there will be no problems.

SECOND NINE

The heavily burdened cart has a place it is going to, so there is no mistake.

THIRD NINE

The duke offers gifts to the Son of Heaven. A lesser man could not do this.

FOURTH NINE

Do not waste strength. There is no fault in this.

FIFTH SIX

The prisoners are bound together and frightened. This means good fortune.

UPPER NINE

He is guarded by Heaven and there can be no question that this is very good.

Going with the Word

Going with the Way –
Let me pause you for a moment
So you can see
That out of this awesomeness
You learn modesty.

What is it? A breath on the wind.
What is it like? Being small,
Surrounded by its vastness, like a wave,
So you know it isn't yours
Or yours to claim –

But you can walk that way
You can become one with it,
And seeing you do this
They can trust you

You are real, then: you're in line,
And you shed that light wherever you go
And then? It holds: it works: it holds.

15

Modesty

Ch'ien

By his offering the nobleman has success.

First six

The nobleman behaves in a modest and humble way. It is good to cross the great river, for this brings good luck.

Second six

Modest speaks for itself. The oracle says good fortune.

Third nine

The nobleman succeeds because he works humbly. This is good.

Fourth six

The retiring and modest cannot but succeed.

Fifth six

He is not wealthy, unlike his neighbours. Now is the time to attack and invade. This cannot fail to be profitable.

Upper six

Modest speaks for itself. Make full use of the army, attack and conquer both the towns and the country.

The Young Son

He is your energy –
Fresh, awake first thing and ready
A clap of thunder rolling over the sky...
And now the clouds, now the promise of the rain
Now, as its first drops fall, is the right time:

Now the rain, flowing in the gutter...
Now the water, not your reason, gleaming on the road –
Now the rain, flowing like the river
Move with it, go with it, from your centre,
So you know like water, silver to strike

From the centre of your forehead and your eyes.
Now is the time, guiding the time,
And being guided – and there is no other:

Be one with the rain, and the river. And move.

16

INTUITIVE ACTION

Yü

This is the right time to set up commanders and move the army.

FIRST SIX

Hearing the elephant, misfortune.

SECOND SIX

As solid as a rock, he does not wait until the end of the day. The oracle says auspicious.

THIRD SIX

To stare at an elephant means trouble. He delays and is very sorry.

FOURTH NINE

Pausing, there is a great haul, so do not question but put the cowrie shells together.

FIFTH SIX

The signs are all of disease and while things are serious, they are not fatal.

UPPER SIX

Powerful forces of the elephant are disturbing. The barrier is breached, no mistake.

Fertile Moon Path

Set off on the right foot
Start right, and there's no problem

                that's the essence

It is time to act – now lead, and follow...
Follow the water to the river, like the river,
Follow on where you are leading, follow it –

Fertile, moon, path: it says

Follow the growing path, the primrose path,
By the light of the moon, and the light of love,
Follow your heart, and follow in the dark
Guided as you are: guidance is on your way

In this moon-shadow-silver reverse of day

17

FOLLOWING

Sui

Original offering. Auspicious oracle. No misfortune.

FIRST NINE

The house is falling down and the oracle foretells good fortune. He is praised for going out and making the crossing which brings fulfilment.

SECOND SIX

He secures the young boy and loses the older man.

THIRD SIX

He secures the older man and loses the young boy. If he hunts he will look and find what he wants. The oracle says, good to find somewhere to live.

FOURTH NINE

Pursue in order to have and to take hold. The oracle is bad. Take hold of prisoners and use in the sacrifice, and what will be wrong with that?

FIFTH NINE

Prisoners attend the festival, good fortune.

UPPER SIX

Caught and bound. Those who follow are caught. The king performs the sacrificial rituals on the western mountain.

Rotten Dick

Deflation: a collapsing sigh,
The hollow truth behind a rictus smile
– mountain-size pieces of rock

flung and following –

The inside of an apple you bite...

And the thing looks great on the outside,
But as soon as it begins to move
You find out the whole thing is rotten:

'The worms have rotted the tool.'

Reality now, scouring. And in you,
It cannot allow you the illusion!
Gain strength from seeing how it really is
Determination, grit and fire
The river!

And it can give you the balls to do it –
When the bubble bursts, and you come down to size.

18

IMPLOSION

Ku

Original offering. It is auspicious to cross the great river. Prepare for three days before starting – for three days after the start.

FIRST SIX

The curse of the father's faults are handled by the son. There are no mistakes. It is dangerous but all ends well.

SECOND NINE

The mother's affairs are in disarray. It is not possible to receive an oracle for this.

THIRD NINE

The curse of the father's faults. There are minor problems but no great trouble.

FOURTH SIX

The curse of a father who has perished.

FIFTH SIX

The curse of a father's failures.

UPPER NINE

He does not work for kings or lords but considers it more worthwhile to work for himself.

The Leader

Closening...
As you walk towards her from a distance,
Or you walk towards your own reflection, feel it:
Alert, attentive with anticipation

How will it be?
Now bring them together, and hold them together,
So they're all under the same roof with you
Hold the tension, and keep walking –
Contain it, and it is enlivening

And by all these mirrored reflections you can see
The broken shards beginning to bind –
And it is the tension you need
Keeping you on its edge. You are closening.

The wave will last for a certain time,
For long enough for it to peak and break –
So set your sights high,

and walk in your feet.

19

CLOSENING

Lin

Original offering, favourable oracle. It says in the eighth month there will be misfortune.

FIRST NINE

Everyone draws near. The oracle is favourable.

SECOND NINE

Everyone draws near and good fortune arises. Without question this is for everyone's good.

THIRD SIX

He is willing to draw near even though this is not a good place. Do not be anxious, the signs are good.

FOURTH SIX

He goes to the very end and all is well.

FIFTH SIX

The nobleman draws near to undertake the sacrifice to the Earth god. This is good.

UPPER SIX

Nothing goes wrong if he draws near. This is good. This brings no problems.

The Eyes of Yin

To look at her eyes
To see their blue shining back
To know who she is
Behind her voice and wavering smile

Kuan...
To look at her with feeling in the silence,

And to see yourself –
To see you are not ready
To see the moment isn't yet right,
And in the mirror of the air
To be able to say
'I am not that light.'

And then, as you lift your palms
They are healing, they are charged
And you can mould the living air around you

And when they see you, they will say
'Here is a man who knows the purity of the Way.'

20

INNERSTANDING

Kuan

The sacrificer washes his hands but does not sacrifice. Be compassionate, dignified and understanding.

FIRST SIX

He studies things like a boy. This is fine for lesser men but is unacceptable for a nobleman.

SECOND SIX

He looks out at things from behind the door. This is good oracle for women.

THIRD SIX

He studies his own offerings in order to decide whether to go forward or retreat.

FOURTH SIX

Study the glories of the kingdom. It is very useful to be the king's guest.

FIFTH NINE

Study your own life. The nobleman therefore makes no mistake.

UPPER NINE

The nobleman – study his offerings and there will be no mistakes.

To the Finish

'Bite the bullet'
But this is no ordinary food
This is food for thought and choosing
And it has been put in your mouth.

You know what to do here: bite through
Savour its difficult taste, and take time
You know the truth of it –
And you need to let it catch up with your mind.

The truth is in your mouth, like blood –
You can't escape it –
What you have done, you have done for it
And if it feels like a prison, remember this:

The truth is the only way out.

21

BITING INTO

Shi Ho

Eating the offering. It is advantageous to rely upon the law.

FIRST NINE

Feet in the stocks. His feet are cut off. Nothing wrong.

SECOND SIX

Biting through skin and cutting off the nose. Nothing wrong.

THIRD SIX

Biting upon sun-dried meat he finds it is poisoned. This is cause for some regret but nothing wrong has been done.

FOURTH NINE

Bites into dried meat on the bone and hits the metal of the arrow. Study the oracle and all will go well.

FIFTH SIX

Biting into dried meat, finds gold. The oracle says danger. Nothing wrong.

UPPER NINE

Wearing a wooden head stock, his ears cut off. This is bad.

The Art of It

Make it beautiful –
Make the moment blossom as it is,
Being with it as it is: do it right
Blending to it from the beauty inside you

It is all here, in the offering
There is nowhere else you need to go
And in its spell of eyes and light

as I see you

You stand in beauty, you stand naturally,
Your bare throat and breasts covered
In a necklace of dry grass thread and cowrie shells
Laid over you

as your eyes shine,

Your head disappearing into the sky...

And as I hang it there, over you, in front of me
Making you out of a picture of the air –
You say 'Honour this as you honour me'

And in the silence of our moment, we are the same.

22

ADORN

Pi

Adorn and honour the offering. There is little advantage in having somewhere to go.

FIRST NINE

Honour his toes, leave the carriage and walk.

SECOND SIX

Adorn his beard.

THIRD NINE

As though honoured, as though anointed. The oracle overflows and brings good fortune.

FOURTH SIX

Adorned as in white, a white horse adorned with pheasant's feathers. Not a robber, a bridegroom looking to marry.

FIFTH SIX

Honour the burial mounds and gardens. The present is small but bound with white silk. Though mean, in the end good fortune.

UPPER NINE

White adornments, no mistake.

Knife

Cut away, break loose
Use the knife –
Free yourself from the fixation,
Free yourself with your eyes

                    it is time –

To free yourself from the binding, and stand.
Cut the good from the bad, the false from the true,
What won't follow will shed and strengthen the rest
And you need strength.

You know about pruning a rose bush, so
This is a different kind of beauty. Freedom.
And you know how water cuts through a bank
Until it loops back on itself in the bow of a lake...

The meaning is plain: it has one root: knife.
As I gesture my hand to you, abruptly, down.

23

FREEING YOURSELF

Po

There is no advantage in having somewhere to go.

FIRST SIX

Cut away the feet of the bedframe. The exorcism oracle is very disturbing.

SECOND SIX

Cut away the feet of the bedframe to clarify. The exorcism oracle is very disturbing.

THIRD SIX

Cut away, no problems.

FOURTH SIX

Cut away the cover of the bed. This is bad.

FIFTH SIX

A string of fish wins the favour of those in power. This is without doubt useful.

UPPER NINE

A ripe fruit which is not eaten means the nobleman gains. The petty people cut away even their own thatch.

Back to your Own

Turn, the oracle says, turn around.

Step out on your other foot, now
In the way you know feels right – tao:
The intuitive foot of your imagining and choosing

Come back to your own kind – and to your roots
Come back into your own rhythm and time –
To the faces that can recognize and greet you,
Laugh with you and heal you, so you can breathe.

Cycles return, seasons, horizons, clouds...
See, it all returns –
This is the Sabbath of your returning
Where you remember who your are
And who you came here to be:

And so I draw you this circle on the ground.

24

RETURN

Fu

The offering goes and returns. There is no need to rush. Friends come and there is nothing inauspicious. He returns to the path. Within seven days will come the return then it is good to go where you must go.

FIRST NINE

The return is not far off, so do not be worried and great good fortune will be.

SECOND SIX

Recover and then return – this is good indeed.

THIRD SIX

Returning beside the river is dangerous. No problem.

FOURTH SIX

Walk alone along the central way when returning.

FIFTH SIX

Return with booty. Nothing wrong.

UPPER SIX

Coming back he gets lost, confused and brings bad luck. There are mistakes and misfortunes if the army is mobilized. Eventually there will be a terrible defeat and misfortune for the ruler and his country. It will take 10 years before things improve.

The One Who Stays

And within this:

> *here is the centre*

> *You – and your truth*
> *And being true to it.*

She is the woman who doesn't run away
She stands in herself and stays
And can you?

What you bring here is what you receive
What you do is what is drawn to you –
And however thin a path it might seem,
If you deviate from it, you're lost...

It's like daring to say the truth, even when
You fling the line uncertain of its response –
But if you stay with it, and hold to your eyes,
You'll get to the other side...

Stay with Heaven, and stand in your height...

And when suddenly it comes

> *screaming overhead out of the silence*

If you stand as you are, I tell you

> *Nothing can harm you.*

25

WITHOUT FALSEHOOD

Wu Wang

The original offering brings a favourable oracle. One who is badly behaved will experience disaster and there is no point in having somewhere else to go.

FIRST NINE

Travel without being false and good fortune arises.

SECOND SIX

Harvested but not ploughed. Farmland but not wasteland. Therefore it is good to have somewhere to go.

THIRD SIX

Disaster can come to those without falsehood. It is like something bound to an ox. The traveller goes and gains. This is a disaster for the urban dweller.

FOURTH NINE

Cast the oracle and there will be no problem.

FIFTH NINE

Illness comes even without there being any fault. Take no medicine but have joyous hope.

UPPER NINE

Even travel undertaken without falsehood can still result in distress and no one place is better than another.

For Everyone

Bounty of the earth:

> *flocks, herds...*

Now abundance is yours, be abundant: use it
But don't just give it out to those close,
Don't waste it at home – take it out
And share it with everyone – anyone
With people you meet – anywhere

> *Harvest sheaves,*

And as you give, you will receive...

Celebrate people, with that light in your eyes,
With every gesture and glancing smile
And together, you can do it
You know we can do it –

> *you can cross the river,*

As great as we are, together

> *like music.*

26

GREAT DEVELOPMENTS

Ta Chu

Favourable oracle, but do not squander it by staying at home. This brings good fortune and it is wise to cross the great river.

FIRST NINE

There is danger. It is best to stop.

SECOND NINE

The axle breaks and stops the carriage.

THIRD NINE

Spur a good horse onwards. The oracle gives a favourable reading of these difficult times. Each day, practise defensive strategies with the chariots, for you may find it useful to go somewhere of your own.

FOURTH SIX

A young bull, yoked, means there will be immense good fortune.

FIFTH SIX

A castrated boar's teeth means good luck.

UPPER NINE

Blessings are the roadway to Heaven.

Eating the Book

Mouthfuls of pages:
Do you know what it is to eat these words?
Then it's not just food you are chewing
But wisdom that can touch your blood
And slake your thirst, and calm your hunger
– your hunger is for what comes first.

Ch'i *of your understanding,*
And the energy around you it energizes, brightening –
The oracles says: mouthful of teeth, and book:
Be moved by what nurtures you, and through it,
Be open to what is given–

                                 this writing

Its marrow made flesh, and the flesh is you.

27

NOURISHMENT

I

The oracle is auspicious. Be moved by that which nurtures. By these thoughts be open to what is given.

FIRST NINE

Ignoring the insights of the divinational tortoise, look at me, your jaws working away. This is bad.

SECOND SIX

A smack in the mouth disturbs the vital energies and to go forward to the attack at such a time is foolish.

THIRD SIX

Unable to take nourishment properly, the oracle says, not good, nor will it be for 10 years and there is nothing good in this.

FOURTH SIX

A smack in the mouth is good for waking you up! It is like the tiger who constantly glares around, for he is driven by the wish to hunt. This is not wrong.

FIFTH SIX

The vital energy is activated and the oracle says settle here. There is good fortune but it is not possible to cross the great river.

UPPER NINE

The starting-point is nourishment but there is danger in good fortune. It is good to cross the great river.

Exodus

The central premise is rotten
the spring beam is sagging...

The whole structure's about to break –
All you know is about to go, so go!

The ground is open and the way is open
For what it falls to, into the unknown.

You must leave what you know.

There's a desert there (look), and a long dry road
No food for miles, and you will have to endure it...

All your strength has been for this

to make you great

Now, use it.

28

GREAT ENDURANCE

Ta Kuo

The house is falling down, so go! This is the offering.

FIRST SIX

Use the white grass for making mats and nothing will go wrong.

SECOND NINE

The withered willow puts forth new shoots. The old man takes a young wife and this is without question good.

THIRD NINE

The central beam is twisted. This is bad.

FOURTH NINE

The central beam is strong, this is good. However, there will be an unforeseen problem. Trouble.

FIFTH NINE

The withered willow brings forth flowers. The old woman takes a young man as her husband. There is nothing wrong in this, nor is there anything praiseworthy.

UPPER SIX

Crossing over the river, water rises above the head. This is unfortunate, but there is no fault here.

No Earth

Edge of the river
> this is where you've reached now:
No earth – only water
> leading to water.

Nothing firm, nothing to grasp.
Nothing to stand on:
> plunged in –

And it's like when you swim
And there's nowhere to rest your feet
And nothing beneath you
> but blue-black sunless darkness

And these depths in your mind.

Now breathe, you are in.
Breathe into the fear:
Swim, swim blind –
You must swim for your eyes.

29

THE WATERY DEPTHS

Kan

The watery depths are doubly dangerous. Have confidence. Bind your heart to the offering and your action will be honoured.

FIRST SIX

The watery depths are doubly powerful. To enter the watery depths of the cave is bad.

SECOND NINE

The watery depths are dangerous. Invocations have little effect.

THIRD SIX

Coming or going, watery depth upon watery depth means danger. Furthermore, going into a cave and watery depth is useless.

FOURTH SIX

A cup of wine, a basket of rice. Two offerings of earthenware pots which are given up to secure the coming of light. At the end, there is nothing to be sorry about.

FIFTH NINE

The watery depths are not full. Heed your own state and peacefulness and there will be no mistakes.

UPPER SIX

Tied down with tough ropes and cords and dumped into a thorn bush for three years means nothing is gained and this is bad.

Skywriting

Bright bird

        soaring above the blackness
      suspended like a single note of sun, SUN

        like a dream,
       a dream of drowning

Your head thrust up from the water –

Sun and moon,
Heaven and earth, together,
Dark and light coming together...

Black cloud above the light
With the sun at its centre –
Like an eye, there ... black cloud
Blazing with the light at all its edges,

      the two clouds coming together...

Dark and light, black and white, deep and bright interfused

– the black in front and the bright behind it
As two sides of the same coin, the same cloud –

Hovering, pausing, waiting, breathing...

And then LI, as the sun spins – LI!
And the whole air rains down brightness.

      You are through.

30

ILLUMINATION

Li

Illumination bestowed by the oracle and the offering. Offer a cow and a bull and good fortune comes.

FIRST NINE

Walking drunkenly. Carry on with due respect. This way there are no mistakes.

SECOND SIX

Yellow and bright: tremendous good fortune.

THIRD NINE

The setting sun loses its brightness, and old people, instead of drumming on pots and singing, tend to moan and groan, and this is sad.

FOURTH NINE

His existence is sudden like a flaring of the fire, which as quickly dies down and is forgotten.

FIFTH SIX

Pouring forth tears, mourning and sighing out of genuine concern. This is good.

UPPER NINE

The king sets out on a military campaign. He shatters the alliance of the chiefs, but in doing so is untainted by their viciousness. This is not a mistake.

2

Cave Mouth, Open Country

No resistance. No opposition.
I see you standing here gazing into the distance,
In the silence, as the wide sweep of the land opens
Blending sand-sea mountains and sky –
                                        waiting.

And there's no one there, no one!
Everything is open in front of you –
Now, embrace it.
Embrace it with your warrior's arms and eyes.

It's all yours – Creation. Life.
It's all yours to be seen in and by...

And as you let her sit up over you like the sky
And you blend to her body, she is Heaven
As you are earth, attentive and firm
– as you close your eyes –

                    Embrace her.

31

FOCUSING

Hsian

An offering ensures a good oracle. To have a wife is also good fortune.

FIRST SIX

Energy in his big toe.

SECOND SIX

Energy in the calves of his leg is bad. To remain is good.

THIRD NINE

Energy in his thighs. Hold the bone. To move will bring troubles.

FOURTH NINE

The oracle says good fortune and all regrets disappear. If uncertain and unresolved in whether to come or go, friends will follow such thoughts.

FIFTH NINE

Energy in his spine means no regrets.

UPPER SIX

Energy in his jaws, cheeks and tongue.

To the End of the Heart

It is a long way over the land
It is a long way over the shifting sands
And everything can change, and will –

But there is one thing that can stay
And that is your heart

>*always walking under you*

Always breathing, always beating inside of you –

And now it says: take it to the limit
– full-blown, like a spinnaker in front of you –
And it will be taken, and tested,
Touched, transfigured, stretched and tormented

Until you know its meaning is real,

>*is All.*

32

CONSTANCY

Heng

An offering, no misfortune. Favourable oracle. Have somewhere to go.

FIRST SIX

Deeply constant. The oracle foretells misfortune and there is nothing to be done.

SECOND NINE

All regret goes.

THIRD NINE

He is not constant in his virtues and some say his offerings are disgraceful. The oracle says, repent.

FOURTH NINE

The field has no game in it.

FIFTH SIX

His virtue is constant. The oracle says, a wife has good fortune, a husband has bad luck.

UPPER SIX

Constant excitement always brings misfortune.

Hidden by Night

What you hide from yourself

> *you hide from receiving –*

So why is it
You are turning away now?
Just at the moment
When you need to stay with it?

You're like a man on the run, in the night
Hiding from the sun and the gold inside you,
Shy so all the best is buried in you.

Face it. Face her.

But to take yourself apart, to be alone –
That is different –
And under cover of yourself, and your eyes,
You can know the true meaning of communing
With all you have to give, and go by, and bring.

Which is it?

33

WITHHOLDING

Tun

Withholding the offering means little is gained from the oracle.

FIRST SIX

The tail is hidden, this is dangerous. Go nowhere.

SECOND SIX

He holds it firm, covered with a yellow bull's hide. Do not remove or take it off.

THIRD NINE

Bound and hidden, this means sickness and problems. Caring for domestic workers and concubines is good fortune.

FOURTH NINE

Hidden goodness in the nobleman is good, but for the lesser man, this is bad.

FIFTH NINE

Hiding excellence, the oracle says good fortune.

UPPER NINE

Hidden wealth undoubtedly brings advantages.

A Sage in a Split Tree

The secret is containment,
Great energy feeding from within.
That's him.

This is what you have, and this is what you need,
But see, of itself

                without wisdom

                        it is nothing.

It is all muscle and brawn,
Balls, brass, fury, and inflation!

Great strength is like a tree,
Its leaves replete in the rippling breeze,
Only the greatest can contain it – Heaven.

The whole sky above you, guiding you.

Do you want to be great? Do you want to be a king?
Then know this. And the thunder is rolling...

34

GREAT STRENGTH

Ta Chuang

Favourable oracle.

FIRST NINE

Strength in the toes. To go ahead would be to incur certain disaster.

SECOND NINE

The oracle says good fortune.

THIRD NINE

The lesser person makes use of strength, while the nobleman does not. The oracle says there is danger. The ram charges the fence and becomes entangled by his horns.

FOURTH NINE

The oracle says good fortune and thus distress fades away. Jump the fence, it will not trap you, for your strength is like the sustaining power of a great wagon wheel.

FIFTH SIX

The ram is lost because of changes, but there are no regrets.

UPPER SIX

The ram who attacks the fence cannot advance, nor can he retreat. Nowhere is he able to gain the advantage. This is difficult but then comes good fortune.

Following the Guide

Now you can go forward: it's time.
Harnessed in strength, like your horse,
As you feel him beneath you, turning and walking,
With your head held up to the sun

> *in sight of everyone,*

And the sun is your source.
Light all around you.
> *They can see it.*

Recognition is yours.

And as one man follows another, all day,
Gaining understanding from him –
See yourself, like your own shadow –

Follow that image every step of the way.

35

PROSPERITY

Chin

The worthy noble subdues. He is offered gifts of horses from which he can breed three times in one day.

FIRST SIX

To the attack, with bravado. The oracle says good fortune. If there is no confidence, keep an open mind and there will be no regrets.

SECOND SIX

To prosper is also to grieve. The oracle says good fortune. He will receive great protection and blessing from the ancestral Queen Mother.

THIRD SIX

All are trusted. Distress disappears.

FOURTH NINE

They are flourishing like rats. The oracle says danger.

FIFTH SIX

Regrets have vanished. Whether you win or lose is no longer important. To go on, that is good fortune and will without doubt turn out for the best.

UPPER NINE

Advancing through use of force he remains true and only punishes the city. There is danger and good fortune. This is not a mistake. The oracle says, there will be regret.

Big Man Bow

Brightness dimmed
> *like the wick*
>> *crouching on its flame –*

the sun setting like a red disc above the horizon
> *about to slip away.*

Call it focusing the beam: the light ray.

When Yi the archer
> *Shot down the seven suns*
>> *One by one with his bow till one was left:*

One was enough for nourishment,
One was all he had room for in his eyes.

And cutting down the brightness means this:
To focus on the centre where the light is falling
Hidden in the darkness

> *reflected in black obsidian*
> *like the pupil in an eye. Eclipse.*

36

DIMMING OF THE LIGHT

Ming I

The oracle says learn from difficulties.

FIRST NINE

The light is dimming, just as a bird in flight dips its wings. The nobleman travels for three days and eats nothing. Whichever place he goes to, the top people speak to him.

SECOND SIX

The light is dimming as a result of a wound in the left thigh. Use a strong horse to help and good fortune will arise.

THIRD NINE

Dimming of the light. Hunting in the South, the rebel chieftain is captured. The oracle says, do not act hastily.

FOURTH SIX

Entering the left side of the belly, reach the heart and dim the light. Leave through the courtyard gate [= breastbone, in Chinese medicine].

FIFTH SIX

Prince Chi dimmed the light. The oracle says this is favourable.

UPPER SIX

No brightness, darkness. First climb to Heaven, then go into the earth.

Shaman Woman

Come home. Listen to the woman now
Listen to her calm, her knowing
– let go to her.

She knows the inside of you
And she knows you belong together.
She knows what binds you –
The whole of her body is that. Listen now.

It is her voice you need to hear.
Her benison, her blessing
That stills the air around you

> *as she looks into her palms*

And the curving grass, the sky and the darting birds
Are one with you –
As you feel the ground beneath your feet
As you gather in, and wait:

> *And now is the circle.*

37

THE CLAN

Chia Jen

The clan benefits from the woman oracle.

FIRST NINE

The home is enclosed. Regrets will disappear.

SECOND SIX

No position. Work from the centre and organize the food. The oracle says good fortune.

THIRD NINE

The clan is full of complaints and threats. If the wife and children are giggling and laughing, this will end in remorse.

FOURTH SIX

Wealthy clan, great good fortune.

FIFTH NINE

The king comes close to his clan. There is no fear, good fortune.

UPPER NINE

Proceed with confidence and with majesty and the result will be good fortune.

Back to Back

You're trying to look at Heaven
Through the back of your head!

You need perspective. You need to stand back.

You yearn upwards, and yet your being draws you down.
You burn, and yet the dark ground won't let you.
You're driven: and your prop-shaft cracks.

You're trying too hard.

Stand back and breathe. Look at the scene.
It's neither of you that's right –
But what lies in between

And if you can see it: it is a levelling
Layered like joy and grief side by side
– the black & white of a fallen feather, blending.

38

STANDING BACK

Kuei

Standing back from minor problems, good fortune.

FIRST NINE

No need for worry. The horse is lost but do not follow. He returns, seeing evil doers. There is nothing wrong in this.

SECOND NINE

Bumping into the lord in the alley-way. No problem.

THIRD SIX

Observe the wagon being pulled along, even though the oxen are restricted. His hair is cut off along with his nose. No beginning, gives an end.

FOURTH NINE

Distant from and alone, he meets the great father. Together in sincerity, they face danger but without regret.

FIFTH SIX

Remorse disappears. The chief ancestor of his family bites through the skin. What is wrong in doing this?

UPPER NINE

Distant from and alone. Observe the pig with mud all over his back. There is a carriage full of ghosts. The bow is at first drawn and then unstrung. He is not a robber but a bridegroom seeking to woo. Go out into the rain and then good fortune will come.

A Mystery

And it's unresolved. You're blocked, again.
You can't go back, that's over –
Even as the past reaches towards you.
And you can't go on

something is holding you

Half-way in the vast limbo space between.

The long dusty road, remember.

And there is a centre, hidden like your belly,
Webbed like the moon among the black of branches,
Occluded, and yet deepening,
Reaching inwards into itself...

Like a mystery you can't yet see.

39

DIFFICULTY

Chien

The West and South are most advantageous, while the East and North are not. It is favourable to see the great man. The oracle says auspicious.

FIRST SIX

Moving ahead is difficult. Coming is praiseworthy.

SECOND SIX

The king's minister faces many difficulties. This is not your problem, it is his concern.

THIRD NINE

Moving ahead is difficult. Come back.

FOURTH SIX

Moving ahead is difficult. Come together.

FIFTH NINE

Considerable difficulties. Come with friends.

UPPER SIX

Moving ahead is difficult. Come to success and good fortune. It is good to see the great man.

Release

Release – again,

       it may be painful, but true.
It is the knife again –

     no change can hold you.

Animal horn, spear, war-axe

       by all these sharp edges
And the sharpness in your eyes that can see
Where you are going, and have to go...

And now: it's like a surge in your blood,
Sudden and unmistakable –
That can sense the nerve of your direction and take it
– stretched as thin as a red line across the miles
So there is no distance, as you feel it –

And it is to the new ground, it must be:

     Nothing less can assuage it.

40

RELEASE

Chiai

The South and West are advantageous. There is no reason to leave. Coming and returning is good fortune. Go to the proper place early on, good fortune.

FIRST SIX

No mistakes.

SECOND NINE

Hunting in the field, catch three foxes. Receive the bronze arrows. The oracle says good fortune.

THIRD SIX

Trying to carry a burden on the back and ride at the same time, allows robbers to attack. The oracle says remorse.

FOURTH NINE

Release your toes. True friends will come.

FIFTH SIX

The nobleman is restricted but achieves release. Lesser people should have confidence.

UPPER SIX

The duke shoots the falcon on the top of the city wall and captures it. There is no question but that this is good.

Giving It

Give out the gift, pour it out like a wound,
Give blood, bone and sinew –
Give love and strength, give it all you have,
And it will return to you:
Your emptiness will be filled.

The gift is for giving – don't hold it back
You can't be a miser and live

But give it mindfully, give it as gold
Glimmering, keening insight, grace
Don't hold back the gift, but the giver
The difference is purity, is this –
Get yourself out of the way...

And then it is not your desire, but its
That gave you the gift to give.

41

GIVING OUT

Sun

Have compassion. Great good fortune. There are no bad signs. Consult the oracle. It is good to have somewhere to go. What is necessary for the oracle? Two baskets of rice should be brought as an offering.

FIRST NINE

Hurry and go from the sacrifice. Nothing wrong. Think and then decrease.

SECOND NINE

The oracle says success. To attack is to court disaster. Not decrease them but increase.

THIRD SIX

Three people journeying together, but then one person is lost. One person journeying, but then he finds his friend.

FOURTH SIX

Control your sickness and hurry up. This brings happiness and no mistake.

FIFTH SIX

People give you 10 tortoise shells and you are not able to refuse. Great good fortune.

UPPER NINE

Do not decrease but increase and there will be no mistake. The oracle says good fortune. It is good to have somewhere to go. Find able people, not just figureheads.

Shaping Up

And after the desert – the city: Life,
The city you have come all this way to enter.

Do you know where you've reached?
Do you know what lies in front of you?

Life has surrendered to you,
Like a cornucopia brimming round you

    like the waters...

        now,

Expand like the river, open your arms –
The barriers, the bridges are down –
What you have been given fills your eyes
And shines like the sun, returning on your face

And it's as great as what you need
For what is coming to meet you
The increase is in you – be awake
To how you need to grow

    to be embraced, by it.

42

INCREASE

I

It is useful to have somewhere to go. It is good to cross the great river.

FIRST NINE

It is good to undertake great actions. Great good fortune and no mistake.

SECOND SIX

People give him 10 pairs of tortoise shells which he cannot refuse. The oracle overflows with good fortune. The king makes offerings to the divine ruler. Good fortune.

THIRD SIX

Advantage gained through making the most of unfortunate circumstances. There is nothing wrong. Be confident and walk the middle way and, using your badge of authority, tell the prince.

FOURTH SIX

Walk the middle way and tell the prince to follow. It is good to make offerings and to be trusted with moving the site of the capital.

FIFTH NINE

There is no question that if you are sincere and kind there will be great good fortune. To be sincere and kind is to be known for your uprighteousness.

UPPER NINE

There is no increase; indeed, there is attack instead. Trying to be moral without a proper code to live by leads to misfortune.

A Forking Path

It says: water dividing
  like the lane

        at its edge

Water, a river, a torrent about to break through –

What are you deciding?
Which way – I'll tell you

As soon as you step, you'll be swept along
In the part of you that already knows

It is the unknown, untrodden path –

    reaching to carve out a new course...

Even as you wait –
Even as your eyes belie it, deny it (if they do):

Stone and river and forking path
– all these cracks in the bone –
And all these images in the dream, are you.

43

DECISION

Kuai

Present it in the king's court. Speak out in trust, even though this will be dangerous. Prepare your own people. There is nothing to be gained from springing to arms. It is good to act now.

FIRST NINE

Strength is in his step. Goes forth but does not triumph. There are mistakes.

SECOND NINE

There are alarms and shouts in the dead of night because of attack. Do not worry.

THIRD NINE

He puts a brave face on it and this brings disaster. The nobleman makes a decision and undertakes it by himself. He walks into the rain and so is soaked through. This is distressing but not a problem.

FOURTH NINE

Bottom rubbed sore, he walks with difficulty. Like a sheep being dragged along, all remorse vanishes. Listen to the words but do not believe them.

FIFTH NINE

Like a strong weed, cut it off and dig it up. Walk the middle way and there will be no regrets.

UPPER SIX

Without advice the end result will be bad.

At One in Herself

Your mouth on her mouth – your hands
On her round, full, ripening breasts
Her arms around your waist; her thighs raised,
And even your tongue, as you dream it, inside her:

But you cannot have her.
You cannot touch what is hers to keep.
Her strong mouth is her mouth, she is other,

For hers is the deep rhythm of water
Where she walks in her way, as she has to, alone

And you? Have to stand like her
And find your whole yearning in yourself
For now or forever

Your own king.

44

MINGLING

Kou

The woman is powerful. Do not, do not marry this woman.

FIRST SIX

Restrained with metal blocks. The oracle says good fortune. Going forth he meets misfortune. A starving pig still leaps around.

SECOND NINE

There is nothing wrong in having a packet of fish. There is nothing to be gained from having visitors.

THIRD NINE

Bottom rubbed sore makes walking difficult. This is dangerous but no great problem.

FOURTH NINE

The packet has no fish. To attack would be bad.

FIFTH NINE

Just as a willow tree covers the melons, so concealing the light comes direct from Heaven.

UPPER NINE

Locking of their horns causes distress but no one is to blame.

Gathering Together

And now, make your offering.
Climb the altar step.
Give thanks, and bow your head.

You have reached your goal –
You have touched the gold
Now everything is gathering round you

    like the day in its lingering splendour

Now, go out – go out together
Go up to the grass, the new pastures,
The new ground, the newfound, Promised Land
Where the sky stretches above you, and the sun blazes...

And as you come slowly down the curve of the field
It is gold silhouetting you, in the one light between us
That has guided us here, as it shows its face...

And as we linger, we know.

        Communion.

45

COMMUNION

Tsui

Communion as an offering. The king approaches the temple. It is good to see the great man make the offering. The oracle says this is good. Offerings of animal sacrifices bring great fortune and it is right to have somewhere to go.

FIRST SIX

Sincerity does not always bring results, which can lead to chaos then to communion. Crying aloud, one embrace will bring smiles. There is no distress, therefore set forth as there is nothing to fear.

SECOND SIX

Led by good fortune, there is no mistake. Faithfully offer the summer sacrifice and this will be advantageous.

THIRD SIX

He communicates with sighs, for there is nothing to his advantage, and nowhere to go. This is not a mistake and brings but few regrets.

FOURTH NINE

Great good fortune and no mistake.

FIFTH NINE

Communion together in the right place is no mistake. If there is a loss of faith, use the original and enduring oracle and sadness will disappear.

UPPER SIX

There is weeping and sighing but there is no mistake.

Vertical

– in this simple action
Of standing up to go

'Ten men, South'

attentive, alert –

And it's in your standing that you find it,
In the gesture you are making –

The origin, the purpose – the whole of it

Rising

now the way is clear

There is nothing between you and its expanse
As the air reaches up above your head
And you can hold the air in your hands

And as the earth rises into your feet
And you know the ground you are standing on
Is as sacred as the ground you are standing in:

Let everything you do be guided by this.

46

ARISING

Sheng

Arising from the original offering. It is good to see the great man. There is nothing to worry about. Attack South and there is good fortune.

FIRST SIX

He arises and is welcomed and great good fortune comes.

SECOND NINE

Have faith, you will benefit from the offering at the summer sacrifices. This is not a mistake.

THIRD NINE

Arise into the hilltop city.

FOURTH SIX

The king offers sacrifices on Mount Ch'i. There is good fortune and no mistake.

FIFTH SIX

The oracle says good fortune. Climb the steps.

UPPER SIX

Arising in the dark. The oracle says, success comes if you strive ceaselessly.

Boundaries

A tree surrounded by a boundary:
You need to enclose your kingdom,

But you don't want to hear it!

You need to make a fortress of where you are
Even as you yearn to go further
On and on over the known world expanding

I can only tell you – you can't.

This is the earth you are on.

Come to ground with what you have
Or else you'll be surrounded –

And if you know what your limits are,
You will use them to anchor your strength.

47

CONSTRICTION

K'un

Make an offering to the oracle and it is favourable for the great man. There is no mistake. He speaks but is not believed.

FIRST SIX

Confined and suffering, his bottom is in the stocks. He enters a dark valley and is not seen by anyone for three years.

SECOND NINE

Confined and suffering amongst drink and food. The official with the red leggings will come. It is advisable to make offerings. To try and push ahead with the attack will bring misfortune. There is no mistake.

THIRD SIX

Confined and suffering by stones. He grasps at thorns. Goes into the palace and does not see his wife. This is bad.

FOURTH NINE

Coming so slowly, confined and suffering within a golden carriage. Sadness will come to an end.

FIFTH NINE

Nose cut off, feet cut off. Confined by high officials. But then, slowly, come words. It is good to worship and make offerings.

UPPER SIX

Confined by creepers. Moves awkwardly and says, 'If I move I shall regret this.' Being repentant, it is possible to move ahead to the attack and have good fortune.

The Deep Centre

And within this

    the centre that is invisible
    the well that the fields surround –

And that is invisible in you
Until you learn to be still,

Being like it.
Close your eyes.

    Don't move, it says,
    Go inside,
    Breathe down.

    See it, now
    Deepening into you
    Down your throat
    And into your belly.

    Can you reach it?
    Does your rope stretch?
    Can you hold it there?

It was always here.
It will always stay –
With its deep dark water.

    Taste it.

48

THE WELL

Ching

The area changes but the well does not. No loss, no gain. Coming and going. The well is. If the well rope is not quite long enough, it will damage the bucket and this is bad.

FIRST SIX

The well is muddied and undrinkable. The old well has no animals.

SECOND NINE

The well has cracked and the fish are leaking out. The storage jug has sprung a leak.

THIRD NINE

The well has been cleaned but it is unused. This makes me sad, for it could be used and water taken from it. If the king sacrifices properly everyone could use it and be blessed.

FOURTH SIX

The well is lined with bricks and there is nothing wrong.

FIFTH NINE

The well has clear cold spring water to drink.

UPPER SIX

The well supplies all who come to it. Do not hide it. Great good fortune.

Stretched Out to Dry

Take your time.
Consider what you've done!
The distance, the desert, the all of it –

It needs to settle, to set, to solidify
And this is the change: it transforms then.

An animal skin stretched out to dry –

a golden bedspread on a washing line

Hung between two branches of a tree...

And when I wear it, you won't recognize me.
And like a new skin, it takes time.

I take my time to be ready. Take yours.
And when your wings are dry

all you'll see is colour, light –

What you've given, for it – and the joy of it.

49

TRANSFORMATION

Ke

Doing so in one's own time. The original offering yields a favourable oracle, sadness disappears.

FIRST NINE

Bound in a yellow bull's hide.

SECOND SIX

Seize the day and change. Go ahead, go ahead and attack to achieve good fortune and there is no mistake.

THIRD NINE

To press ahead with the attack brings bad luck. The oracle says danger. He discusses three times and then changes, when he has enough confidence.

FOURTH NINE

Sadness disappears. You will win and it is a good time to change course.

FIFTH NINE

The great man takes on the tiger's persona. Before undertaking the divination, make sure you know what you are doing.

UPPER SIX

The nobleman takes on the leopard's persona, while lesser men simply change the appearance of their faces. To go ahead with the attack is bad luck. Stand firm and the oracle says good fortune.

Offering Up

And can you let it go?
Can you let it be beyond you?
Can you offer it up?

It is hidden in your heart, and your heart knows
This is the sacrifice, and you are it.

Feel it. And it is burning
With the clear flame we call love
That burns off what doesn't belong to it.

Feel it, and it is a jewel
It is the most precious thing you have.

And it is yours – because you gave it.

The flame burns rose in your mind, like wine.

It is the best you have, and you gave it. Can you?

50

THE SACRIFICE

Ting

Sacrificial pot. The sacrifice is the fundamental origin of blessing.

FIRST SIX

A sacrificial pot overturned. To exorcize evil is to your advantage. A concubine is useful because she can give a son. There is no mistake.

SECOND NINE

The sacrificial pot is full. My colleagues are ill but they cannot harm me. Good fortune.

THIRD NINE

The handles on the sacrificial pot have been changed. Actions are stopped. The pheasant's juices are not eaten. The rain comes and there are problems. In the end, there is good fortune.

FOURTH NINE

The legs of the sacrificial pot are broken. The duke's rice has been spilt. He is mutilated as punishment. This is bad.

FIFTH SIX

The sacrificial pot has yellow ears and gold rings. The oracle says good.

UPPER NINE

The sacrificial pot has rings of jade. This is great good fortune and all is very advantageous.

Losing It

And the centre is in this too:

  that despite the dam-burst of rage –

  despite the rain coming in through the roof

  despite the wind banging open all the doors

– at the drained end of the cup of loss
A perfect circle with a dot appears:

And something in you is so still
That you jump, but don't jump
You listen evenly –
As you breathe, and survey the scene

And as the door bangs, you continue
– or it continues in you
As empty as you are, jetted through
Translucent as your face appears

So you can see that the spoon he holds
With its ruby red liquid doesn't even tremble...
Because he knows all he has left is true.

51

TRAUMA

Chen

Make an offering, for traumas are very disturbing, yet he is chatting away and laughing. The trauma strikes fear into those for 100 miles around, yet not a drop of sacred wine is spilt from the spoon.

FIRST NINE

The trauma causes fear, real fear. Then comes chat and laughter, real laughter. Good fortune.

SECOND SIX

The trauma brings danger. His fortune is lost. Go to the ninth burial mound. Do not go looking, for in seven days he will be found.

THIRD SIX

Nervous, very nervous after the trauma. Journey on and there will be mistakes.

FOURTH NINE

Trauma and then there is mud.

FIFTH SIX

The trauma makes people come and go, which is dangerous. Losing your fortune is not a real disaster, for you have a career.

UPPER SIX

The trauma causes anxiety, real anxiety. Casting around in fear, real fear. To attack is disastrous. The trauma affects those around him but not himself. There is nothing wrong in this, though within the family there will be gossip.

Siddhis

'Hold, stop, cease, contain' – and then breakthrough
Break through into the power of stillness and silence
As you find it in you: amazed, like a ghost –
But awake and alive, more than alive –

And look at him: he walks in the courtyard
He is so still that no one can see him
As a white feather drifts down from the air
As white as him

        or as you,

          freed of your usual body

And three thousand years later, he is standing there
Surrounded by the crowds who came to see him
Who do not even notice him as he glides past
As light as the breath of that feather on the air –

And everywhere and nowhere but in himself, at one.

52

STILLING

Ken

Stilled in himself, but not limited by his body, he enters the courtyard but is not seen by anyone. There is nothing wrong in this.

FIRST SIX

Stilling his feet, there is nothing wrong. The oracle says this is good.

SECOND SIX

Stilling his legs, he is no help to his companions and he is disquieted by this.

THIRD NINE

Stilling his waist and meditating upon his own centre, the spine is dangerous and his heart burns with excitement.

FOURTH SIX

Stilling his body is not a mistake.

FIFTH SIX

Stilling his mouth makes what he says worthwhile and sadness disappears.

UPPER NINE

Still and integral, good fortune.

Rolling

The wagon rolls,
The rock has been entered

    – we're coasting on the freeway –

And teach your soul
How to fly
From the bird

        as it floats on the thermals

To flow with the wind, like water –
Like the movement of your body as you walk at ease
In step with yourself and your feet
Or as you run and feel the breeze on your face,
Free now

      the sea drifting like a great mirror

     its waves rippling, dreaming...

Not forcing the hand of anything
Or of her, as she lies with you now
Your will, or her desire –
And then it is all open, all breathing

    and this is the New Life tao.

53

COASTING

Chien

The woman is ready to marry. The oracle says this is good.

FIRST SIX

The wild geese coast into the shore. The younger son is in danger and there is gossip. But there is no mistake.

SECOND SIX

The wild geese coast towards a cliff, where they eat and drink happily, really happily. Good fortune.

THIRD NINE

The wild geese coast towards the plains. The husband goes to war and does not return. The wife is left pregnant but unable to care for the child. This is all unfortunate. Defend yourself against robbers.

FOURTH SIX

The wild geese coast towards the trees, landing in their branches. Nothing wrong.

FIFTH NINE

The wild geese coast towards a mound. The wife, married three years and still not pregnant, eventually achieves what she wants and settles down. This is good fortune.

UPPER NINE

The wild geese coast towards high land. Their feathers can be used for certain rituals. Good fortune.

Immaturity

Your feet on the ground,
You're wearing your cap,
You're calling at the house –

But she's not ready. She's out.
She's not ready to say yes. She can't.

Anima, puella, sapling – symbol
Of a marriage that would be a disaster –
And she's not ready, because you aren't either –

She is in you, mirroring you. Own her.
She is the unripe apple, the hasty scheme
That confuses the dream with the growth it needs

As the world wheels by with its ephemera
Along its hoarding of transient images

in a world where nothing lasts

And nothing is what it seems...

54

MARRYING THE YOUNGER SISTER

Kuei Mei

It is disastrous to attack and there is nothing to be gained anywhere.

FIRST NINE

Marrying the younger sister off as a secondary wife. The lame can walk, so go ahead. A good time to attack.

SECOND NINE

The one-eyed can see and the prisoner's oracle says this is for the good.

THIRD SIX

Marrying the younger sister into a lowly position, she returns however as a secondary wife.

FOURTH NINE

The younger sister is almost past marriageable age, but though late, the marriage will happen.

FIFTH SIX

The Emperor Yi gives his younger sister in marriage. Her dress is not as fine as that of the other wives. The moon is nearly full, good fortune.

UPPER SIX

The woman carries a basket with nothing in it. The youth sacrifices the sheep but there is no blood. This is of no use at all.

3

The King

Harvest time now. Bleached light on the fields
And the whole earth gathered in plenty –
Imagine the abundance, it is yours,
You have enough. You can breathe.

The cup is full of wine as you raise it,
Above it are two sheaves of corn...
Now this is the apex, this is the throne
To stand in what is royal in you –

The light everywhere, to your left and right,
The sun still on its wheel of fire,
All flame become light, and the light, gold
So you know the glory that is I

                                  for a moment

Where you stand beyond time as you close your eyes
And all you know is the blazing gold
That fills you, reaching down to your feet
And fusing the ground with the sky

       And it is not your will, or mine.

55

SOVEREIGNTY

Feng

Make the offering. The king draws near and there is no sadness for this is proper like the sun at midday.

FIRST NINE

He meets his lover but only for 10 days. There is nothing wrong. Go ahead and you will have your reward.

SECOND SIX

His prosperity is like a thick curtain. At the equinox he can see the stars of the Dipper. To go ahead will be to court suspicion. Have faith and act according to this and you will have good fortune.

THIRD NINE

His prosperity is like a flowing banner. At noon he can see the smallest stars. He breaks his arm but no one is to blame.

FOURTH NINE

His prosperity is like a thick curtain. At the equinox he can see the stars of the Dipper. He meets his equal and this is favourable.

FIFTH SIX

The various aspects come together and there is reward, fame and fortune for the long-term future.

UPPER SIX

His home is prosperous and he cordons off his house. Peering out of his door, there is no sound, no people. For three years he sees no one. This is bad.

After Li Po

Where do you come from? Where are you going?
It is not the world as you see it –
I have different eyes from yours

And I cross your path like a shadow.
What is it you really need?
What is that weight around your shoulders?
Who gave you that complacent smile?

I know a different kind of kingdom
Where all I carry is the sky and the moment
And people are as they are, like me,
And birds and bees and flowers are equal.

Fool, minstrel, tramp – I am all of these
But my secret is I am no one
And the breeze that blows through me is the breeze
And my vanishing breath on the wind.

What I give, I give. It is all I have –
And the miracle is that it's enough.

56

THE TRAVELLER

Lu

The traveller makes a small offering. The oracle says, to the traveller, blessings.

FIRST SIX

The traveller breaks up what is settled and causes upheaval.

SECOND SIX

The traveller arrives at an inn. He hides his wealth and uses young servants. The oracle says to the traveller, auspicious.

THIRD NINE

The traveller burns down the inn and loses his young servants. The oracle says danger.

FOURTH NINE

The traveller rests and finds his treasures and an axe. My heart is not at ease.

FIFTH SIX

He shoots a pheasant and the arrow disappears. Eventually he is praised and honoured.

UPPER NINE

A bird burns down its own nest. The traveller starts to laugh but then weeps and cries. Because things changed he lost an ox. This is unfortunate.

Letting Go

Let go, give over,
Be like the breeze
Gentle and penetrating –

Be like a whistling song.

Don't hammer the air around you.
You don't have to yell to make yourself heard.
And what melts my heart in laughter
Could melt yours, if you'd let it.

And where there seems no way, the way comes
When you both agree to it:
'We're stuck – what can we do?'

And then look, it breathes

     as the leaves ripple in the silence

And you find yourself in the Garden

     where you belong...

57

YIELDING

Sun

Make small offerings and it is good to go where you want to and to see the great man.

FIRST SIX

Advance or retreat? The oracle tells the soldier what is good.

SECOND NINE

Yield and make the offering below the altar. Use bards and shamans and other similar people. Good fortune, no mistake.

THIRD NINE

Always yielding and offering means sadness.

FOURTH SIX

Distress vanishes. In the field, hunting brings three different kinds of catch.

FIFTH NINE

The oracle says good fortune. Sadness disappears and this is obviously good. No beginning, but there is always an end. Three days pass before things change and this is then followed by a further three days. Good fortune.

UPPER NINE

Yield and make the offering below the altar. He loses his wealth. The oracle says bad.

Sing Out

Open the window to that music
It's catching the beat inside your body
In spite of you, isn't it?

Sun, moon, mountain, kingfisher-moment:
It's all for our delight,

> *didn't you know?*

Trust where the line breaks
The mould breaks
And where your energy wants to go –

Have you ever seen an oracle get up and dance?
Well, you have now.

58

DELIGHT

Tui

Make the offering and benefit from the oracle.

FIRST NINE

Harmony and delight, good fortune.

SECOND NINE

Confidence and delight, good fortune and sadness disappears.

THIRD SIX

Desiring delight brings misfortune.

FOURTH NINE

Pondering upon what brings delight does not help him. In a distressed state, he has delight.

FIFTH NINE

He trusts in division and this is dangerous.

UPPER SIX

Seductive delight.

UPPER NINE

There is victory from drinking wine, this is not a mistake. But if you get drunk, you may be caught and the sacred spoon taken.

The Sower, The Reaper

Paper on the breeze,

                 the coins falling...

Seeds where the wind takes them

                      the weather, broken.

What picture is shaken into the sand now?
What can you see? What are you feeling?

Awash in the change that erases these –
Fragmentation, the force of water,
Flooding, sweeping and cutting loose again
Irresistible change

               expanding

And only something inwardly settling to ash.

It is not in your hands anymore.
It is free, it is natural, it is itself.
Come home to yourself now, go back to the source
Where you came from, across all your journeying

And it is this: it has to be your own,
And all you have is this floating world...
– a handful of seed for the wind, as your fingers open.

59

SCATTERING

Huan

To make the offering the king comes to his temple. It is good to cross the great river and benefit from the oracle.

FIRST SIX

He uses a strong horse to rescue. Good fortune.

SECOND NINE

The sacrifice splatters the altar and sadness disappears.

THIRD SIX

Scattering over his body, no sadness.

FOURTH SIX

Scattering over the group brings excellent fortune. Spreading over the mound is something of which no ordinary person would think.

FIFTH NINE

Scattering sweat, he cries out greatly. Spreading over the king's palaces, there is nothing wrong.

UPPER NINE

Scattering his own blood. Go afar off out of here. No mistake.

Measuring

Gathering in your hands, your thoughts, your speech.
Bringing the walls in around you.
It is a natural turning, an inflection
Considered in the notches of the bamboo measure.
It is your rule, your length and extent.

And the oracle says: be gentle
Measure the time with an eye for inches
And build that ground from your dwelling –
But don't build it so tightly at the other extreme
That it becomes a clenched prison you can't

get out of –

Measure your restraint beside your breathing.

60

RESTRAINT

Chieh

Make the offering. The oracle advises, restraint should not be too severe.

FIRST NINE

He does not go out of the door or the courtyard. No mistake.

SECOND NINE

He does not go out of the gate or the courtyard. Mistake.

THIRD SIX

No restraint leads to distress, make no mistake.

FOURTH SIX

Peaceful restraint is an offering.

FIFTH NINE

Sweet restraint brings good fortune. Proceed and you will be praised.

UPPER SIX

Harsh restraints. The oracle says this is bad. Sadness disappears.

On the Nest

Be true to yourself
In the house of yourself
And see how you come out falsely –

See you're aching to leave it
And you are longing for it

                                 and see this:

You have to dwell inside to know the difference,
You have to live in your own heart first.

Consider the hen
Brooding over her eggs,
Confident and assured – the root says

And centre in as you did in the beginning,
To where you can say No and Yes –
In the one place you have to return to

That is in you, and everywhere, then.

61

KNOWING

Chung Fu

Suckling pigs and fish, good fortune. It is good to cross the great river. The oracle is favourable.

FIRST NINE

Favourable for burial offerings. Having distractions means no peace.

SECOND NINE

A crane calls out from her shady hide. Her chicks answer back. 'I have a full cup and will share it with you.'

THIRD SIX

He meets his opponents. Perhaps drumming, perhaps stopping. Perhaps weeping, perhaps singing.

FOURTH SIX

The moon is almost full. One of a pair of horses disappears. There is nothing special about this.

FIFTH NINE

The opponents are caught and bound. This is not a mistake.

UPPER NINE

The sound of the cockerel rises to Heaven. The oracle says bad.

Down to Size

The lark soars

                    and plummets, free-falls,

Landing alert with his head up –

And it's the small things that matter supremely
Which come to meet you on your path.

Do you ignore the tiny desert flower?
Are you a hero treading on a snail?

I tell you, in the end, it is life that matters
In each moment of your responding –
Life, and love: not power.

We've had enough of all that now.

And all the long road into the future is this:
Can you live as if everything mattered?

                Then you will live.

62

THE SMALL THINGS

Hsiao Kuo

The offering brings a favourable oracle. Consult for minor issues; do not consult for major issues. A bird on the wing sings its song. It is not right to go up, it is better to go down. Great good fortune.

FIRST SIX

The bird on the wing is a sign of bad luck.

SECOND SIX

Going beyond his grandfather, encounters his grandmother. Failing to reach his lord, encounters his officials. No mistakes.

THIRD NINE

Do not go beyond the walls in order to chase someone who is armed. Bad.

FOURTH NINE

No mistake. Do not go beyond, confront instead. To go out is dangerous, be careful. There is nothing to be gained in the long run by asking the oracle.

FIFTH SIX

There are thick clouds coming from the West but no rain falls on my lands. The duke fires and takes those in the cave.

UPPER SIX

Do not go beyond; avoid instead. The bird on the wing is trapped, bad luck. A sign of disaster and distress.

Ending

NO TRUMPET BLAST –
No shout of hurrah –
And little left to learn
But what you already know:

It's over, it's already over as it was.

Long talks and late nights trying –
It has all been dying into completion
Line by bottom line ... unstoppable in the silence,
Now all you have left is the letting go

You are human, and alone. Put on your black clothes.

And as the sun sets on the endless road,
The dream is what the dream was. Raise your eyes:

A new seed of dawn, a new day is beginning
When all you see now will be nothing. Nothing.

63

FINISHED

Chi Chi

***The offering brings a moderately good oracle. At
the start, good fortune; at the end, chaos.***

FIRST NINE

His wheels drag; his tail is wet. No mistake.

SECOND SIX

The wife has lost her jewellery. Do not rush after the jewels,
they will be found in seven days.

THIRD NINE

The Great Ancestor attacks the Ghost regions. It takes three
years to subdue. Lesser men should not attempt this.

FOURTH SIX

The leak is patched up with cloth. Be on guard all day long.

FIFTH NINE

The neighbour in the East sacrifices an ox, but this is not as
good as the neighbour in the West's summer sacrifice, for this
brings great blessings.

UPPER SIX

His head is wet, danger.

Over our Heads

AND ALL YOU ARE will be dust
All you have will be lost
Your empire will corrupt
Like all of the rest –

You cannot stop the sun

    from moving over your head

And in the letting go: I see you as you are
In freedom, as I did – I see you again –
As two bright sun-clouds merge above our heads...

And the young cubs roll and yelp in the yard

        in the half-light,

And none of this is over, not yet,
Not a word of it written – none of it
The day, the dawn, is only just beginning
That the earth is waiting to inherit

Take off your black clothes. Didn't you know?

    The Book of Life is never closed.

64

UNFINISHED

Wei Chi

Make the offering. A young fox, while crossing the stream, gets his tail wet. Nothing is going well.

FIRST SIX

His tail is wet – sadness.

SECOND NINE

His wheels drag. The oracle says good fortune.

THIRD SIX

He has as yet to cross the stream. It is a bad time to attack. Good for crossing the great river.

FOURTH NINE

The oracle says good fortune. Sadness disappears. Disturbance leads to an attack on the Ghost regions. In three years he is given rewards by the Great Country.

FIFTH SIX

The oracle says good fortune. No sadness. The nobleman's glory arises from his sincerity. Good fortune.

UPPER NINE

So full of confidence, wining and dining. There is no mistake. Nurturing this, he gets his head wet and he does not achieve what is right.

2

MODERN
COMMENTARY

Modern Commentary

1 The Origin
Ch'ien

The Way is the Way for all life. It is the origin of the Origin. Combining Heaven twice (the trigram for Heaven is three straight lines and there are six straight lines in the hexagram), it is pure yang and brings good fortune and success. It is most auspicious.

The dragon symbolizes pure yang. When all is well, the dragon is soaring and leaping. When things are not well, the dragon is held down by the waters – the yin of life. Through the proper functioning of the yang, all is held in balance and prospers.

First nine Do not do anything at present for the energies are low.

Second nine A time for the reserving of powers until an appropriate opportunity comes, then all will go well.

Third nine Continue to use your skills wisely and despite set-backs, you will succeed.

Fourth nine This is a restless line, not content to be where it is. Resolve this and all will go well.

Fifth nine The dragon is like the Emperor, above all others. Seek the guidance of one such as this.

Upper nine Do not overstretch yourself, for such action will lead to regret and distress.

All nine The yang forces reach their peak and are at their most powerful, but also about to descend.

2 THE RECEPTIVE
K'un

As Ch'ien is pure yang, so K'un is pure yin. From these two comes all life, even Heaven, Earth and humanity. From yin, the submissive one, comes the power of the Earth. Things rise to Heaven from the Earth, whereas Heaven can only descend to Earth. While K'un is submissive, it rises as a result of its submission. It triumphs through gentleness, hence the image of the sound or sturdy mare.

FIRST SIX Discern the signs of the times and be prepared for things getting worse.

SECOND SIX All is balanced and in order and therefore you can achieve what you have set your heart upon.

THIRD SIX Do not expect instant results but work steadfastly. As a result, skills will be acknowledged and honour gained.

FOURTH SIX Yin is not active like yang. It holds in and keeps secure that which it has and therefore no difficulties arise.

FIFTH SIX To wear imperial undergarments shows what a high position the wearer has reached. To be in such a position is to have very good fortune.

UPPER SIX With yin at its strongest, the world is in danger of tipping over into terrible disaster. Only by holding the balance with the yang can the natural cycle be restored.

ALL SIX If the proper balance is maintained and used in an honourable way, then only advantage can come from these lines.

3 BIRTH PANGS
Chun

This hexagram is made up of the trigrams for thunder and water, which stand for Heaven and Earth, man and woman. They are opposites and although it is possible for them to live in harmony, this can just as easily tip over into strife. It is like birth, full of opportunity but also fraught with danger.

The final line means 'Seek advice and guidance from those whose whole way of life reflects order and continuity', i.e. hereditary rulers. This hexagram is a warning not to start anything lightly.

First nine There is little one can do in this position other than be sensible and look for help from those above.

Second six Do not allow things to be rushed by others. Take time to consider and act appropriately. Time will bring its rewards.

Third six Do not venture into areas beyond your experience. Be like the ideal man who either seeks advice or does not press ahead.

Fourth six Problems will arise at the start of anything. Seek help when necessary and all will be well.

Fifth nine People in positions of authority should bestow favours in minor ways, quietly. This will not cause problems. Those who insist on the grand gesture will stir up resentment.

Upper six All is coming apart. The grand plan has failed. Retreat and bemoan what has happened.

4 THE ADOLESCENT
Meng

The heart of Meng as a hexagram is a mess of lines – some broken, some complete. The character Meng shows a house with parasitical plants growing from the roof. The whole emphasis is on the mixed up, lanky, parasitic and inexperienced young person who is impetuous and even rude. The two trigrams represent the mountain resting on water – inherently unstable.

But all is not lost. If the shallow youth can learn from both the wisdom of the diviner (the 'I' of the text) and from his own mistakes, then eventually he will grow up. But it is not easy.

First six Use punishment with great care. It can be helpful for curbing the wilder excesses of the young, but it can also rebound. The young should not be unduly constrained.

Second nine The secret of success is a contented home.

Third six Do not fall for those whose only interest is money. No good will come of it.

Fourth six Surrounded by ignorance, your life is bound to be a disaster. Free yourself from such constraints.

Fifth six Through honesty and innocence, good fortune can come to even the young.

UPPER NINE When you are confused and feel threatened, do not resort to violence but try to find your way forward, carefully.

5 PATIENCE
Hsu

The two trigrams are water and Heaven. The rain of the water is yin while the heat of Heaven is yang. With these combined, life can flourish. But growth, fed by rain and sustained by sunlight, is not a quick thing. It takes time. So it is with Hsu. Patience is what is needed. All our needs will be supplied, but if we rush, we shall fail. Patience, allow things their own good time.

FIRST NINE Be patient, in no hurry to arrive. If you can be patient, all will work out well.

SECOND NINE The sands, just like the whims of the common people, are always shifting. Hold fast to what is true and you will have good fortune.

THIRD NINE These are sticky times and the slow journey you must take leaves you vulnerable. Take care.

FOURTH SIX It is as if this line is a tomb, a place of death and blood sacrifice. If you do not move on, life will cease to be important to you.

FIFTH NINE Traditional offerings to the gods include wine and food, so you will be rewarded for your efforts.

UPPER SIX This is a dark and difficult time and the unexpected occurs. Be patient and polite in all circumstances and all will be well.

6 DISAGREEMENT
Sung

The two trigrams combined to make Sung are Heaven in the upper trigram and water in the lower trigram. The two natures do not go together easily, for the Heaven trigram is like a ruler or high official who tries to establish firm laws on something as fluid as water. The character Sung means a legal dispute or disagreement and this is reflected in the text. Compromise – don't go to the bitter end. Go to the judge, the great man.

Don't set out on some major venture at present such as crossing the great river. Act cautiously, testing each step rather than rushing at things.

FIRST SIX This line basically means agreement, so don't allow minor issues to cloud your judgement.

SECOND NINE When defeat faces you, get away as fast as you can and go to where you can guarantee support and friends.

THIRD SIX It is not fashionable to value tradition or to act as a gentleman, but this is the right way.

FOURTH NINE Your fate is partly yours to determine and partly fixed by Heaven. If you are unable to make your own way, stop struggling and observe what Heaven has decreed for you.

FIFTH NINE This line is like an honest judge who ensures that a case, properly conducted, is successful.

UPPER NINE You may win your dispute but such gains are transient and it would be better not to even start.

7 THE ARMY
Shih

There is only one full line in this hexagram, for the top hexagram is earth and the bottom is water. It is around the pivot line that the hexagram finds its strength. This pivot is represented in the character Shih, which consists of a mass of people circling a central pole. Thus an army is only as good as its commander.

The hexagram symbolizes both the need for a leader and the fact that a leader will arise when the need arises.

FIRST SIX To follow rigidly what you are told is to fail to understand. This way leads to defeat.

SECOND NINE This straight line is the pivot line – the command line – and around this everything else circles.

THIRD SIX Don't keep a commander who is useless. Find a new leader or disaster will strike.

FOURTH SIX Conserve your energies and be tactful.

FIFTH SIX Your enemy is open to attack, but beware! It may be a trap and you will find you need an experienced leader, not someone who is too young to know the rules of the game.

UPPER SIX It takes the great to act in an appropriate way. Anyone less than this is simply not able to get the best out of a situation.

8 UNITY
Pi

The only full line is one down from the top and is therefore in a commanding position, but only because the other lines support it. The two trigrams are water and earth – very auspicious because they produce life. But life only flourishes when the conditions are at their best. So do not tarry but grow and develop when the opportunity arises. To do this, co-operate, for the divinatory readings are good.

FIRST SIX By turning your enemies into your friends you can have success.

SECOND SIX We can only work well with others if we know ourselves.

THIRD SIX Do not continue to associate with bad influences.

FOURTH SIX Look beyond yourself and your close friends.

FIFTH NINE By hunting only on three sides the king allows the strongest animals to escape and breed more healthy creatures. But the city folk don't understand this. Be like the king and allow the best to continue rather than force all to do your will.

UPPER SIX Do not forget the need for a leader.

9 RESTRAIN THE LESSER
Hsiao Ch'u

Wind and Heaven combine here, making a wispish, highly mobile hexagram which can cause problems because it lacks substance, hence the call to restrain the lesser.

There is potential here: heavy rain-bearing clouds sent from Paradise – the West is the Land of Paradise to the Chinese – but no rain actually falls. The time is not yet right, so do not allow things to come to a head yet. More time and more important developments need to take place.

FIRST NINE You have been led astray. Return to the true path and all will be well.

SECOND NINE Returning to the true way is not easy – but it is worth the struggle.

THIRD NINE Life is becoming complicated and things that should run smoothly have become entangled. It is no good trying to avert your eyes and pretending that nothing is going on.

FOURTH SIX This one yin line is vulnerable – but be calm and keep your integrity and all will be well.

FIFTH NINE Unity is important, especially so if you are to share money or capital of some sort.

UPPER NINE A dangerous time when what has gone before is in jeopardy. Be cautious.

10 WALKING CAUTIOUSLY
Li

The two trigrams are Heaven and the swamp or lake. But Li is important as a hexagram itself because it stands for virtue and lies at the heart of Chinese philosophy about human nature. The tiger refers to the wild, uncivilized side of human nature, such as was manifested in the last Shang Emperor, while Li refers to civilized, moral behaviour. The need to assert Li over the tiger element bespeaks the fundamental struggle within each person and within society.

FIRST NINE Behave correctly and virtuously and all goes well.

SECOND NINE All conditions favour you if you act wisely.

THIRD SIX You may be better now, but do not go beyond your strength. That way lies pain and misfortune.

FOURTH NINE You are in troubled times. Be cautious.

FIFTH NINE This is a good time but be careful.

UPPER NINE If you study what is happening and act in accordance with the way forward, you will be very fortunate.

11 BENEVOLENCE
T'ai

The two trigrams are Heaven and Earth. Combined with humanity, you have the Great Triad, the very essence of Chinese cosmology. T'ai symbolizes this, being the name of the most sacred Taoist mountain, a site hallowed for millennia and where the Emperors went to receive the blessing of Heaven, Heaven's mandate to rule and represent the Earth.

This hexagram, carrying the two main yin/yang trigrams, denotes great opportunities for those who know how to balance the forces and work with them.

FIRST NINE In eradicating a nuisance, other more valuable but intertwined elements will also have to go if you are to be successful.

SECOND NINE Work with what comes to you: be patient and straightforward and hold true to the balance of forces.

THIRD NINE To have yin, you must have yang. The vagaries of life make life possible.

FOURTH SIX Yin and yang can lead a person into oscillating pointlessly between them. You may seem confident, but really you are unable to control things.

FIFTH SIX Male and female should complement each other and play their appropriate role.

UPPER SIX If you are not constantly prepared, you will fail and your destiny will be beyond your control.

12 BLOCKED
P'i

This hexagram contains the trigrams for Heaven and Earth, but reversed from no. 11. Thus it is the negative, the opposite of Hexagram 11. This hexagram means the reversal of the natural order, the blocking of the flow of energy. It is the sign under which the true Way is upset. So even the wise man, the sage, can do little. The true rulers, the great ones, are overthrown and the lesser people arise.

This is not a time to do anything. It is a time when the forces of the world are out of control.

First six Set a good example and others will follow – set a bad example and the same will happen. Therefore, act correctly.

Second six Remain true to what you believe and allow those below you to have their day, but within certain limits.

Third six Learn to live with what is past.

Fourth nine This line is a good one. Be straightforward and accept your place in society and contentment will be yours.

Fifth nine Be wise enough not to try the impossible. Instead, retire gracefully.

Upper nine Although the odds were against you, the way is now clear or can be cleared if you really try. But don't expect instant results.

13 ALLIES
T'ung Jen

The two trigrams are Heaven and fire and they go together well, just like allies or comrades in arms. The potential inherent in such a grouping is good and should be used or put to some specific purpose. The hexagram rests upon its yin line and this is a good sign, for strength lies in the five yang lines and flexibility in the one yin line.

First nine True friends always join you and those whom you welcome to your home are the ones to work with.

Second six Do not form alliances which divide the family.

Third nine Things are not going well and you are preparing for the struggle – but bide your time.

Fourth nine Be prepared and you will be able to survive.

Fifth nine Do not launch any major venture until you have the resources you need, properly marshalled.

Upper nine Look for allies and assistance wherever you can.

14 ABUNDANCE
Ta Yu

The two trigrams are fire and Heaven. Here the combination is a good one, for from such a union comes fruitfulness. The term 'Abundance' has the connotation of being wealthy and that such wealth is to be used communally. The fire above Heaven means the light which lights Heaven – very auspicious. It also means that the power of fire – so destructive – is mediated through the benevolence of Heaven.

FIRST NINE Caution is needed. If you practise this, the rest will come easily.

SECOND NINE Plan well and all goes well.

THIRD NINE The Son of Heaven is the Emperor. While a rich man can make gifts to the Emperor, a lesser one would be ruined. If you have wealth, use it properly.

FOURTH NINE Use your gifts carefully, don't waste them.

FIFTH SIX This one yin line brings all together. If you share wealth or skills you can become powerful.

UPPER NINE Do not take your wealth for granted. It is only Heaven's blessing. Remember this and you will do well.

15 MODESTY
Ch'ien

The two trigrams are the earth supported by the mountain. Although the earth is a stronger trigram, it does not mind being supported by the mountain. Such is modesty. This is a peaceful and generous hexagram, signalling power held in abeyance and opportunity given to others. Trust in those who are below you and your trust will be returned.

FIRST SIX Be very modest – humble and modest. This is the way to proceed if you are to undertake great tasks.

SECOND SIX The modest person never has to shout about his or her achievements. You will be known for what you are.

THIRD NINE Be as modest as possible, for this is a dangerous line. If no one notices you, you will do well.

FOURTH SIX You will succeed if you act properly and without fuss.

FIFTH SIX Modesty does not mean weakness. Be prepared to act when really necessary.

UPPER SIX If you have been true to yourself and humble, then when you need to act, you will find others who will join you. Do not hold back, but go all out.

16 INTUITIVE ACTION
Yü

The two trigrams are thunder above the earth. This is a good combination, for thunder rolls freely over the earth. The hexagram signifies flowing easily with the forces of life. If you are to be successful you need to flow easily, going with the tide, but also be sure that this is what is right for you. Just as the earth is greater than the thunder and thus accommodates it, so you must learn that authority needs to be acknowledged and then action taken.

FIRST SIX This is a weak line, so be careful in all your actions.

SECOND SIX Do not follow others but be true to yourself and act when you know you should.

THIRD SIX Looking trouble in the face can be unnerving, but if you hesitate all will be lost.

FOURTH NINE This is a time for consideration and for taking stock of what you have.

FIFTH SIX Take great care.

UPPER SIX There is great power in the flow of life – not always for the good. Changes may be needed to avoid disaster.

17 FOLLOWING
Sui

The two trigrams are the lake resting upon thunder. They accommodate each other and follow each other's lead. The thunder brings rain which creates the lake. The lake is often the place over which thunder breaks. So they follow one another for both are dependent upon the water they share between themselves. This hexagram means mutual concern and interaction.

FIRST NINE The world is changing. Those who seize the initiative will do well.

SECOND SIX Be innocent rather than clever.

THIRD SIX Choose the way of wisdom and knowledge.

FOURTH NINE No time to be soft. If what you want is to happen, others will suffer. Have you thought of that?

FIFTH NINE This is the Emperor line and means you should trust your superior.

UPPER SIX You are all bound up together and should seek to survive through mutual care and concern.

18 IMPLOSION
Ku

The trigrams are the wind bearing the mountain. This is a very inauspicious hexagram. A wind bearing rocks is like a typhoon smashing everything before it. The character, Ku, shows a pot full of crawling creatures – poisonous or sinister. This is not a good hexagram. However, careful preparation and the passage of time does bring renewal, recovery and rebirth – but only after decay and loss.

FIRST SIX For a son to sort out his father in imperial China meant things had become very bad. Extreme measures are called for to maintain order, yet these very measures bring change.

SECOND NINE There are some people who, no matter how close they are, you are unable to help because of the intimacy of the relationship.

THIRD NINE Hold back. A few losses are better than chaos.

FOURTH SIX Bury the past: praise what was good and move on.

FIFTH SIX You are still burdened by the past. Handle this first.

UPPER NINE Look to your own affairs and don't worry about the world.

19 CLOSENING
Lin

The two trigrams are the lake or marsh, supporting the earth. This is a very good combination, for the moisture rising from the marsh nourishes the earth and brings forth life.

Lin has a powerful set of meanings, including 'to be friendly', 'to descend' and 'to draw near'. It has the sense of a new but exciting relationship. But there will be testing times and such a union needs to set itself achievable targets.

FIRST NINE There are two yang lines which support each other. The support of good friends is vital for success.

SECOND NINE Solidarity and resoluteness are the secrets. Do not yield to fads and everyone will admire you for this.

THIRD SIX Be cautious. The situation is very difficult, but act properly and all will be well.

FOURTH SIX The union line between the trigrams. All now goes well.

FIFTH SIX Be sensible and give authority to those who deserve it and all will go well.

UPPER SIX All is at its best and things will go well.

20 INNERSTANDING
Kuan

The trigrams are the earth supporting the wind. This is a good combination. The hexagram title, Innerstanding, indicates that in such a union of earth and sky, true knowledge of one's self is called for to discern the right way to move. Humanity is the bridge between the worlds.

The two trigrams illustrate the way a wise person affects the world. Like the wind, he moulds and moves people to the right actions. Likewise, the grass or trees, as they bend in the wind, not rigid and thus breaking, show us how to live.

FIRST SIX Do not act like a child. Be your age.

SECOND SIX You are only looking at things in a very sheltered way. You cannot make a decision on that basis.

THIRD SIX Know yourself to find out what to do.

FOURTH SIX Try to understand by placing yourself in the shoes of the other person.

FIFTH NINE Know yourself.

UPPER NINE Look for guidance from those who know.

21 BITING INTO
Shi Ho

This is a very powerful and rather awesome hexagram. It brings together Chen in the lower part, thunder, and above it Li, fire. This is where the imagery of the mouth shutting and the jails slamming shut come from. To be caught between thunder and fire is to be in considerable difficulty! The notion of jaws clamping shut is reinforced by the righteousness of these jaws. For they bite down upon sacrificial meat, thus showing that what they are doing is just and right.

This image of fierce but just action is reinforced by the unusual appeal to legal authority and power in the second part of the ancient text. The character for 'law' or 'litigation' shows the character for 'dog' repeated twice with the character for 'shout' in between. This again reinforces the idea of being caught between two forces. The notion of having no way to avoid the consequences of actions runs strongly through this hexagram and the whole text emphasizes the righteousness of just but severe action – as understood by the harsh Chinese penal code.

FIRST NINE Beware of forces that can oppress you, so reform your ways.

SECOND SIX Do not cut off your own nose to spite your face. Be careful and thoughtful in your actions.

THIRD SIX Not everything goes as intended, but perseverance and faithfulness will succeed.

FOURTH NINE Bite the bullet, confront the problem and all will eventually work out.

FIFTH SIX Beware unexpected material benefits. The sage says these corrupt.

UPPER NINE Do not be surprised by punishments for having done what was wrong.

22 ADORN
Pi

The trigrams here are mountain and fire and the hexagram reflects the supportive nature of the mountain to the fire. While the fire may destroy the grasses and trees, it can never damage the mountain. Indeed, the fire at the centre of the

Earth produces many mountains, and the fire on the mountain can create new soil for plants to flourish in. It is as if the two adorn and honour each other in this hexagram, mixing the yang lines with the yin in a very supportive way.

In this text the meaning of 'adorn' or 'honour' is linked to the sense of the fulfilment of nature, its adornment being a perfectly natural aspect. Thus the person asking a question of this hexagram is advised to be like nature and to change or honour as the time dictates.

FIRST NINE Treat even the most lowly with respect and proceed in peace.

SECOND SIX Do not waste time on eternal changes when the real change needed is internal.

THIRD NINE This is a good line. Treated with respect, all will go well.

FOURTH SIX Sometimes outward show can be sign of sincerity. Learn to judge when this is so.

FIFTH SIX Paying respect, in however small a way, shows the right attitude.

UPPER NINE White, the Chinese colour of death, calls for quiet reflection on the real purposes of life.

23 FREEING YOURSELF
Po

This hexagram combines the trigram for earth at the bottom and that of mountain above. The combination would seem to be a good one, for surely mountains come from the earth. But there is a fundamental weakness here: the five lower yin lines serve to weaken the one yang line at the top. In a similar way, that which can seem firmly rooted and secure can be found to be unstable and subject to movement and change. This is also referred to in the title 'Po' – freeing yourself.

The character combines two other characters, that for a knife and that for cutting. It also has overtones of divination sacrifices. The meaning is clear: to discover the true nature of anything, even something as seemingly permanent as a mountain, cut away and free yourself.

First six Beware of doing something without firm foundations or good advice. If the advice urges caution, follow this.

Second six Examine a situation critically and seek good advice. If the advice urges caution, follow this.

Third six Simply cut away all that obscures and study what really exists.

Fourth six Take care lest you so over-examine something that you destroy it altogether.

Fifth six This line defers to the upper yang. Use your discretion to find assistance.

Upper nine The wise are provided for, while those who cannot comprehend the larger picture destroy even their own basic shelter.

24 RETURN
Fu

This is the hexagram which distils the essence of the Tao and is reflected in Chapter 40 of the *Tao Te Ching*, but bear in mind that this is not the full-blown Tao of parts of the *Tao Te Ching*.

The trigrams of thunder below and earth above are co-operative, but the heart of this hexagram lies in its sense of the cycle of coming and going, of return to the centre and of continuity. The five yin lines resting upon the firm yang line show this to be a stable hexagram, and the image of seven days refers to the wish of the Chou dynasty to introduce a seven day week, always returning to the same firm base. There is a strong sense of what we would call *metanoia*, meaning 'to turn around completely', 'to be saved or changed'.

First nine Be patient and all will come together and there could be nothing better than this.

Second six Collect yourself before attempting any restoration and you will then succeed.

Third six There is no going back. Keep on and things will work out.

Fourth six Remain true to your Way and do not fear being alone. Those who can manage this centredness will succeed.

FIFTH SIX Walk tall and proud along the right way and you will do well in life.

UPPER SIX If the Way of Heaven is reduced to chaos, then disaster will strike. In such circumstances, do not attempt to move or initiate anything, but wait until the disruption is over – no matter how long.

25 WITHOUT FALSEHOOD
Wu Wang

This hexagram opens with exactly the same four characters as the first hexagram, yet it enhances or adds to what was said then. The notion of original offering and oracle is expanded to illustrate the point that such an oracle is only really possible to those who follow the true path and do not debase themselves.

The trigrams are Heaven above and thunder below. This hexagram carries with it the idea of Heaven's judgement or retribution on the unjust, those who threaten the order or Way of Heaven (remember here that Way used here does not refer to the fully fledged Tao of the *Tao Te Ching*).

The hexagram also carries with it the notion of being prepared for the unexpected, a thunderbolt out of the blue. But it also says that the person who is consistent and faithful to the truth need have no fear of such events.

FIRST NINE Be true to yourself and you will find that things work out well.

SECOND SIX Sometimes there are rewards even if you have done nothing to earn them. Take advantage of this.

THIRD SIX Troubles come to even the innocent and one person's gain is often at the expense of another.

FOURTH NINE Be still, think and even if things are not going well, this will help with any further problems.

FIFTH NINE Misfortune can come for a multitude of reasons. The best medicine is joy and celebration, so treat the whole spirit not just the particular sickness.

UPPER NINE There are times when it is best to stand still. Even actions performed for the best of reasons can bring unexpected distress.

26 GREAT DEVELOPMENTS
Ta Chu

The term 'Great Developments' tries to capture the sense of the original characters, which signify the holding of a vast array of domestic animals and all the farming consequences that entails. It is to be seen as a distinct improvement on or development from the wandering herdsman or nomadic existence from which the Chou arose and from which the Chinese were always pulling people into their civilization and from which they were also frequently under attack. The skills of domestication and farming were, mythologically, bestowed at the beginning of Chinese history by the great legendary ruler Fu Hsi, who 'discovered' the Eight Trigrams.

The two trigrams are Heaven at the bottom and mountain on top. This gives the sense of a greatness of Heaven focused upon a sacred mountain, such as Mount Ch'i, a place where revelation and instruction were received.

The reading indicates that those who have great herds and (therefore) wealth should not be frightened of putting it to work, either by seeking new pastures or new fields to work in.

The idea of seeking a divination about whether to migrate or not is fairly common in Chinese texts, and the reading seems to encourage movement, not staying at home. All goes well for those who use their Great Developments.

FIRST NINE Even though the venture you are engaged in is good, there are times when you need to stop and think.

SECOND NINE Normal progress can be frustrated by the simplest problems. Solve them first before pushing on.

THIRD NINE Do not be frightened of going forward. Be prepared and ready and willing to move on.

FOURTH SIX If you are ready to move and have all your things in hand, then things will go very well.

FIFTH SIX To tame what is wild and to make it serve you is the best way forward, not least in dealing with your own self.

UPPER NINE Through seeking advice in a proper, humble way, you can be guided.

27 Nourishment
I

The two trigrams, mountain above and thunder below, give a hexagram which resembles a mouth filled with teeth. This seems to be the source of the association of this hexagram with nourishment, with what the jaws grind up.

There seems to be a deliberate pun upon the notion of the divination. Many divinations were made by animal sacrifices, such as the turtle or the ox or sheep. Thus you can be fed by the oracle at two levels. The first is that it gives you an answer to the question you put – so you are fed at the 'spiritual' level. But it was also common to then eat the sacrifice and thus commune with the gods and with blessing in a very organic way. It makes a clear link between the sacredness of being and the being of sacredness in anything, including our food. We are nourished at different levels.

FIRST NINE If you disregard the spirit and concentrate upon the material, you make a bad mistake.

SECOND SIX You are under pressure and shaken up. This is no state in which to take drastic action.

THIRD SIX Those who are frightened of what will be revealed or discovered will never benefit from instruction or revelation which can illuminate others.

FOURTH SIX Disturbing incidents and events can be turned to advantage if they alert us to what is going on and stimulate us to respond more decisively.

FIFTH SIX Events shake you up and stimulate you, but do not tackle anything too big at this stage. Find your base.

UPPER NINE You may have what you need to feed you, but is it doing more damage than good? Watch what goes in, for this affects what you can do. Be aware of this and you can tackle even the greatest tasks.

28 Great Endurance
Ta Kuo

This hexagram brings together the marsh at the top and the wind below. This speaks of fluidity and movement. Nothing is certain or fixed. All is subject to change and decay.

The message of this hexagram is that you should not put your trust in anything which seems solid but can break. Instead, be ready to change and to move as things change. In particular, even if the very centre of your being, of your security – here symbolized by the central beam of a Chinese house (which were generally one floor only so if the central beam went, the house collapsed) – seems weak, change everything and move on. But do not expect any long-term security in a world of wind and marsh, for it cannot provide this.

The term 'Ta Kuo' also carries the sense of great experience and of considerable insight or survival, beyond that which is normally expected.

First six Just as in Chinese divination you start by kneeling on such a mat to seek guidance, so prepare yourself humbly before every venture. Put yourself in the right frame of mind.

Second nine Even that which seems past it or dead can spring to life again. Look again at what you have.

Third nine Those who think of themselves as central, pivotal and strong are wrong. Their weakness can bring the house down.

Fourth nine What you have as a core is good. Do not try to replace it with something else.

Fifth nine While there is nothing wrong in what you plan, it will not bring the fruits or rewards that you might have expected.

Upper six Taking risks is not a bad thing, but neither is it necessarily particularly wise.

29 The Watery Depths
Kan

This hexagram is made up of the trigram for water, repeated. In ancient Chinese the repetition of a character serves to give extra emphasis to its significance. Thus the waters become the doubly deep waters, the particularly deep or powerful waters.

This is not a hexagram to take lightly, for it could sweep you away and draw you down into the watery depths where humans cannot survive. It is necessary to be like the two yang lines of the hexagram: although trapped within the waters, if they remain true to what they are, they can survive. In part this comes from being able to bend, to flow round things. The water image of the later *Tao Te Ching* is evoked here, but with an edge of danger in the water itself.

FIRST SIX Do not get out of your depth. This is particularly stupid if you can see from the start that this is dangerous.

SECOND NINE You should be very careful, for not even prayer can help you if you go in too deep.

THIRD SIX Whichever way you turn, danger confronts you. Don't even try to find somewhere else, for this will be as bad. Stay still and hold on.

FOURTH SIX By doing what is right, following the proper procedures and seeking help from those who can shed light on what is happening, you can escape this predicament.

FIFTH NINE Leave well alone.

UPPER SIX Like it or not, there is little you can actually do for some time to come.

30 ILLUMINATION
Li

This hexagram consists of the trigram for fire, twice. In Chinese thought, two similar things are often used to symbolize a particular attribute. Thus, the character for day and that for moon, when put together, mean 'brilliant'. So with these two fires, we get 'brightness, illumination'. In fact the two words 'brightness' and 'illumination' are very closely linked in Chinese.

The references to sacrificial offerings, divinations and cows and bulls marks this clearly as being a text concerned with balancing the forces of nature so as to create a workable harmony which will sustain life. Furthermore, the cow stands for the domestic and the bull for the wild. In such a harmony, fire is a maverick. It is a vital component of civilization but it is also one of nature's great destroying forces. Fire is both promise and threat. This is why the hexagram talks of both a cow and a bull – no one force, yin or yang, can be allowed to dominate.

FIRST NINE Pull yourself together, stop behaving as you do and get your act together.

SECOND SIX Yellow is the colour of the Emperor, of the Earth. It is the colour of brightness. This is an auspicious sign; you are blessed.

THIRD NINE All things come towards their end. But it is up to you whether you go out in a blaze of glory or in a petty, grumbling way.

FOURTH NINE Life is, ultimately, brief and then gone. So do not concern yourself with what is ephemeral.

FIFTH SIX Reflecting upon the realities of life, one is often moved by great sadness. Do not harden yourself. Let the tears come and you will more fully understand the nature of existence.

UPPER NINE You may have to take certain drastic actions to contain the envy or cruelty of others. But do not in your turn become a tyrant or marred by their methods and thinking.

31 FOCUSING
Hsian

This hexagram combines trigrams for the marsh at the top and below it the mountain. This is a good combination for the moisture of the marsh creates the pastures on the sides of the mountain and from the pastures flow the rivers which supply the oceans which provide the rain to fall upon the mountains. Thus is the cycle of life maintained.

This is why the text mentions how good it is to marry, for in the harmonious living of man and woman and their begetting of children, the cycle of life is likewise continued. The mountain needs the marsh and vice versa. The wise man or sage has knowledge but also listens. The man and woman likewise need each other to complement and complete each other. Hence the title, Focusing, to focus on, to shape or to influence, for this is what we all need to bring out our completeness.

FIRST SIX When you first stretch in the morning, it is your big toe that moves first. Now is a time for new but modest beginnings.

SECOND SIX Ignore the desire to travel. Stay put.

THIRD NINE Stay put, do not follow the lead of others.

FOURTH NINE The reading is good, so do not hesitate or

ponder any more. To do so will be to mislead your friends.

FIFTH NINE You are keyed up and excited, hence the tingling of the spine, but all this is for the best.

UPPER SIX Words can be false even when spoken with great force. Weigh words and see whether they ring true.

32 CONSTANCY
Heng

What, in the thinking of the *I Ching*, is constancy? For the 'Book of Changes', constancy is the inevitable change and transformation of all life at all times. This is what is constant. But it is harnessed in this hexagram to the particular character, Heng. One half of the character is made up of the character for 'heart'. It is the heart which offers its own form of constancy in the constant change of life.

The two trigrams united here are the wind below and thunder above. The wind blows where it will, showing that the foundation of constancy is ever-changing, and the thunder strikes where it wants and cannot be predicted in its course. Yet against this, the other half of the character for Heng shows either a boat moving between banks or the moon moving between horizons. This signifies either a boat moving downriver, going with the flow, or that the moon rise and set is a constant. So the hexagram seems to be posing a conundrum of what it means to talk of constancy in a world of change.

FIRST SIX Caution. Do not invest too much in that which is bound to change.

SECOND NINE Let this speak to the reader.

THIRD NINE Those who fall from being constant in those aspects of their life which shape their behaviour will be censured and should reform.

FOURTH NINE You cannot catch that which is not there. Do not set out on some great venture unless you are sure of its outcome.

FIFTH SIX This is a very good line for women. Do what you have been asking for. Men should hold back.

UPPER SIX Do not waste your energies. Hold fast to what is true.

33 WITHHOLDING
Tun

The trigrams in this hexagram are Heaven above and the mountain below. The image here is of a person turning their back on what they should be drawn to or respond to. Thus someone on a mountain top naturally turns to Heaven. Yet the reading seems to indicate someone who is at a religious event but who takes the sacrificial food and hides it instead of offering it up. This results in Heaven's favour being withdrawn and the oracle is thus able to say little.

On the other hand, those who seek to truly understand Heaven will retreat to a mountain top to better contemplate what Heaven wants. This is to hide from the masses, which can bring openness to Heaven.

FIRST SIX Beware and remain where you are.

SECOND SIX You have been given power and authority. Use it and use it well.

THIRD NINE Outwardly, all seems well, but there is an inner sickness which cannot be disguised. Learn to consider those you normally ignore.

FOURTH NINE The lesser person has to boast, whereas the wiser person keeps quiet about his good deeds.

FIFTH NINE Modesty brings its own rewards.

UPPER NINE Modest bearing – hiding the riches of your personality – brings greater rewards than bragging and boasting.

34 GREAT STRENGTH
Ta Chuang

This hexagram both warns against the false use of great strength and celebrates the prowess of great strength. In other words, great strength by itself is useless or even dangerous. It is the purpose to which it is put that makes it meaningful or otherwise.

The two trigrams are Heaven below, with thunder above. This speaks of the immense power in Heaven, especially in the destructive power of thunder and lightening. When Heaven directs thunder and uses it to warn those who err, the its power is meaningful. But when Heaven is not involved and thunder simply rumbles forth, then it has no moral significance. The powerful only have true meaning when guided by moral, ethical and spiritual insights to which they bend their strength.

FIRST NINE Even though there seems to be power moving you forward, resist.

SECOND NINE There is nothing to add.

THIRD NINE The fool rushes in, the wise person does not. Do not get into confrontation, thinking you can use your power to win. You will not.

FOURTH NINE Get going. You can clear all barriers and move implacably onwards to your goal.

FIFTH SIX You may have lost your strength and your way, but this could open up new opportunities. Do not panic.

UPPER SIX Stuck in a particular mode of response, you are going nowhere. This is a hard time to live through, but you will realize the futility of what you are doing and change, and then new possibilities will arise.

35 PROSPERITY
Chin

The hexagram is formed from the trigram of fire above and earth below: in other words, the sun rising over the earth. The hexagram focuses upon the rising of fortunes, but always carries also the message that just as the sun must set, so does fortune. There is also a strong theme of fecundity here, emphasized by the breeding horses. Prosperity means increase – not just in inanimate objects but also in offspring, domestic animals and workers.

This theme of prosperity is closely linked to the success of a ruler. The whole hexagram speaks in imperial, often military terms. Thus, if a king does well, so do his people. If a noble does well, this is because his emperor does and this then reflects well on the rest of the country.

Mutual advancement is here implied – but always with the edge of decline, the yin of the yang.

FIRST SIX Success and disaster are two sides of a coin. Remain open even in times of distrust.

SECOND SIX Life is a cycle of ups and downs. Learn to hear the voice of the wise woman.

THIRD SIX Establish trust and your problems will dissolve.

FOURTH NINE Your problems are growing and growing. Step carefully.

FIFTH SIX There is nothing to add.

UPPER NINE You may feel justified in taking drastic action, but it is not the right way.

36 DIMMING OF THE LIGHT
Ming I

The characters for this hexagram's title are intriguing. The meaning of Ming is 'brightness', consisting of the characters for sun and moon. The character for dimming is made up of a man with a bow. This signifies barbarians, outsiders, those whom the Celestial Empire felt had to be subdued. Yet there is also a connotation of the glittering pheasant.

The image is the reverse of the previous hexagram. Here the strength is declining and falling away towards the darkness, just as the pheasant is often seen flashing its colours at dusk. There is therefore the notion of decline. This is borne out in the trigrams. Fire is below earth, the sun is setting. The cycle of growth, strength and thus decline and weakness is the essence of this hexagram.

FIRST NINE You are coming to the end of this trial or journey. Prepare yourself by reserving your energy.

SECOND SIX You are in trouble, but it is solvable. Draw upon those who can support you and all will go well.

THIRD NINE Success may seem to be yours, but remember the rise and the fall of power. Take time to assess the situation.

FOURTH SIX Painful as it will be, you must go to the heart of the problem and confront it. There will be no easy solution.

FIFTH SIX Prince Chi, a nephew or grand-nephew of Emperor Chou, was the last surviving member of the Shang dynasty overthrown by the Chou. He was spared so that he could continue to offer his imperial ancestors sacrifices, thus ensuring they did not disturb the kingdom. In times of greatest tribulation, you may still survive, even if it is in a reduced state.

UPPER SIX This is the cycle of the sun. You must learn to rise and to set. This is the Way of Heaven.

37 THE CLAN
Chia Jen

This hexagram combines wind above with fire below. More importantly, it focuses upon the home and the clan. The ancient text has usually been translated to emphasize the domestic and subservient role of women in the clan. This is explored in the lines. However, it can also be read in the light of the major role played by women shamans from whom the oracles often came. We have gone towards that reading of it. It says, in essence, listen to the wisdom of the woman oracle and learn from that.

FIRST NINE A family needs structures and a sense of order. This will help resolve certain difficulties.

SECOND SIX By being humble and working hard to provide what is necessary, you will find fulfilment.

THIRD NINE Control may be unpopular but it is better then disorder.

FOURTH SIX If all things work together, then all is well.

FIFTH NINE Go towards your problem, not away from it. Take your responsibility on your own shoulders.

UPPER NINE Be confident in your own power and rights and act accordingly.

38 STANDING BACK
Kuei

The two trigrams united here are fire above and marsh below. They do not mix and thus emphasize the title, Standing Back. Furthermore, they each produce flickering, moving images, indicating the uncertain state. The eye cannot be sure what it is seeing, nor the mind really know what to make of the strange shapes thrown up by firelight or the spectral images created by the fog of a marsh. All is not as it seems. We are distant from these images and it is in this distance that we can hope to discern the real from the unreal.

FIRST NINE Follow the Taoist way of no-action. Let things be.

SECOND NINE Unexpected help will come, if you can recognize it when you meet it.

THIRD SIX Beware. This complex reading carries a warning, so do not try to do anything at present.

FOURTH NINE Be guided by one whom you can really trust. Ignore all others.

FIFTH SIX Your family's past now intrudes into the present. Learn from this.

UPPER NINE All these images are of omens of fertility, fecundity and unexpected fortune. All is strange and uncharted, but you will succeed.

39 DIFFICULTY
Chien

The two trigrams here are water above and mountain below. This image captures the nature of difficulty. The mountain seems at first so much greater than the water. Yet over the years, water wears away the mountain. It is similar to the images in the *Tao Te Ching* of water flowing round, under and eventually through the hardest rock. This is what this hexagram is about. It is about finding the right way, learning how to deal with apparently insurmountable difficulties, even if the advice at first seems to be turning you away from confronting them. Flow with the Tao.

FIRST SIX Do not try to force your way. Retire and reconsider.

SECOND SIX Judge which difficulties are really your concern.

THIRD NINE Return to basics.

FOURTH SIX Only through working with others can you progress.

FIFTH NINE Rely upon your friends.

UPPER SIX Take advice; resist the temptation to dash ahead.

40 RELEASE
Chiai

The trigrams are thunder above with water below – a storm. Like a storm, we have the potential for sudden explosions, releases of energy, anger or enthusiasm which can invigorate us or leave us exhausted. Either way, such releases are often painful, even if their end result is beneficial. The character shows this in that it is made up of other characters depicting knives and sharp horns. The implication is that a release comes through the use of something violent or potentially dangerous, but used in this instance for the good.

First six A weak line but one which carries no blame. Remain still.

Second nine All is set to go well.

Third six Do not try to do too much, otherwise you will fail badly.

Fourth nine Stop being so tense. Let go and allow your friends to help you.

Fifth six Trust in those who know better.

Upper six Difficult as the task may be, do not waver but look as to how you can do what you must do.

41 Giving Out
Sun

Here is a clear shamanistic text giving details of how to prepare for a reading or sign. The two trigrams are the mountain above and the marsh below. The whole thrust of this hexagram is that only by giving appropriately – decreasing what you hold by pouring out – can you hope to receive back. Thus offerings made to the oracle seem at one level a waste. Yet they will bring back advantages which cannot be equated with simple material goods.

There is also the notion of controlling desires and wishes – a pouring out or decrease of the ego in order to be an emptier vessel into which Heaven can pour its own blessings.

First nine Have you taken on too much? Stand back, consider and then act.

Second nine Hold back from your planned action. Your vigour will only help your opponent.

Third six Just two is what nature prefers. Three bring discord and distress.

Fourth six Get a grip on yourself and on your future.

Fifth six Tortoise shells are used in divination. Thus friends give you advice which should be heeded.

Upper nine Find true friends and good workers, not just those whom others think you should listen to.

42 INCREASE
I

The two trigrams here are wind above and thunder below. Both are moving forces which carry things forward. This underpins the image of increase – increase in action, in progress towards goals and so forth. All the imagery is of movement, of moving from one place to another and of overcoming barriers. The notion of movement and progress runs through this hexagram.

FIRST NINE The ideas you have should be followed through.

SECOND SIX What you plan is blessed.

THIRD SIX Make the most of what befalls you.

FOURTH SIX What you are considering is a vast step. Make sure you can carry all those you need with you.

FIFTH NINE No need for further comment.

UPPER NINE Is what you want to do guided by some higher purpose? If not, then do nothing.

43 DECISION
Kuai

The two trigrams here are the marsh above and the Heavens below. The hexagram therefore has five yang lines rising up to meet the one yin line. They look ready to break through, to make a decision to overthrow the yin line. This is a hexagram of potential and of opportunity. This is further emphasized in the character, which should have the sign for water on its left. This has become lost over time. The notion of water and the rest of the character, meaning 'to part' or 'fork', means the full character indicates a river ready to push forward and to carve a new course. So this hexagram is welling up, ready to break forth and make a decision.

FIRST NINE You are being too rash. Do not just go where your emotions lead you.

SECOND NINE Be on your guard.

THIRD NINE You are faced with clearing up someone else's mess. Do so and you will be blessed, even though it will be difficult.

FOURTH NINE You are being drawn into something you should not be. Stop, go no further, even though it is likely you will want to ignore these words.

FIFTH NINE Your problem is deep rooted. Only by radical action can you deal with it.

UPPER SIX Listen to what people are saying to you.

44 MINGLING
Kou

The two trigrams are Heaven above and the wind below, two forces that mingle in themselves, both being in the sky. The character for this hexagram has a double level of meaning. It can mean 'to meet' or 'encounter', but it also has the strong sense of sexual intercourse. Hence I have used the term 'Mingling' to convey something of both. It could be translated as meaning 'Intercourse with a strong woman – do not marry such a woman'. This is a strange hexagram with some very difficult and odd lines in it, harking back to very basic oracles and perhaps to a renowned woman shaman.

FIRST SIX This is a line which urges caution, so do nothing precipitate.

SECOND NINE The packet of fish represents pregnancy. Therefore this is a time when you should take care of yourself and not be troubled by others unduly.

THIRD NINE You are in a poor shape, so take things slowly.

FOURTH NINE A time of infertility.

FIFTH NINE What is to be is hidden, but the promise is of marvellous confluence between what you wish and what Heaven desires.

UPPER NINE Do not try to do things on your own nor clash with others unnecessarily.

45 COMMUNION
Tsui

The trigrams are marsh above and earth below. The waters which flow into a marsh stay there, forming a mass of unmoving, intermingled waters – a gathering or communion of the waters. The earth supports this. Likewise, offerings and rituals performed on Earth commune with the gods and with Heaven, gathering together to form a spiritual blessing and resource for those who have joined in the rituals. In order for us to have communion with Heaven, it is necessary to offer something from ourselves and of ourselves, following the right procedures and listening carefully to what Heaven says in response. This is the communion betwixt us and Heaven.

FIRST SIX You are sincere but this is not enough. You also need human warmth, otherwise what you plan will fail.

SECOND SIX You should be open to the forces around you and should pay heed to them.

THIRD SIX This is a time of sadness and inactivity. Do not try to force the pace, but wait for better times to come.

FOURTH NINE There is nothing further to add. \

FIFTH NINE The time and place is right, but you lack faith in your ability to do what must be done. Return to your roots and listen to the message of the divine sphere that comes from these roots.

UPPER SIX This is a sad time, but that is as it must be. You will come through.

46 ARISING
Sheng

The two trigrams are earth above and wind below. As such, the wind ascends through the Earth and goes to Heaven. This whole hexagram is related to communion between humanity and Heaven. It is about actions which, through their virtue, arise as hymns, prayers or actions to Heaven. The emphasis is on developing those characteristics which speak of devotion to Heaven and which appear manifested in action.

FIRST SIX Move forward and you will find you are welcomed.

SECOND NINE The summer is a time of growing towards the light. Do what is right and proper and you will grow.

THIRD NINE What looks like an honour will turn out to be hollow and meaningless.

FOURTH SIX Do what is right and start to put things right where you live before venturing further afield. Be in touch with your roots.

Fifth six Go ahead with your plans.

Upper six Times are difficult, but never waiver from doing what is right, no matter how tempting offers may be.

47 Constriction
K'un

The two trigrams here are marsh above and water below. This means that progress is greatly restricted. You are surrounded by yin influences which totally dominate the scene. Hence the notion of confinement and distress which this hexagram carries. It is one of the most depressing of the whole book. It offers little in the way of encouragement, other than to follow what the former hexagram is saying, which is that you must be in a proper state of devotion and prayer if you are to survive. It emphasizes the need to be in communion with Heaven, rather than rely upon your own strength or cunning, which frankly, in this situation, will be of little use.

First six You face humiliation and you will have to learn how to live with this and find your way back again to self-respect.

Second nine Await those in authority coming to you. Do not try and precipitate things.

Third six A barren time. Do not try to hold onto things which are useless, but learn to value that which is really central to your life.

Fourth nine You are trapped by what you have. Realize this and your suffering can be broken.

Fifth nine There are things you have done which have now exacted punishment. Learn from this and behave properly.

Upper six You have got yourself into this. Acknowledge your mistakes and then change can occur.

48 The Well
Ching

The two trigrams are water above and wind below. The whole theme is of the interaction between humanity and nature. A well is a controlled natural spring. As such, it is a collaboration between humans and nature. But if humans move away, the well, or more precisely the spring, continues, whether humans make use of it or not. The symbol of the rope which is too short only emphasizes this. Nature gives, but human stupidity can fail to make proper use of this, to the advantage of no one. The rope stands for the failure of humanity to work in accord with nature.

FIRST SIX What you are trying to keep going is no longer worth the effort.

SECOND NINE That which you expect to sustain you is in danger. Make repairs, do not ignore the problems.

THIRD NINE Things may seem fine, but because of ignorance or laziness, all is far from well.

FOURTH SIX Things are in good repair. You are making the best use of what you have.

FIFTH NINE You are in a good situation. Make the best of it.

UPPER SIX Draw support from nature and rejoice in what is given to you by nature, not what you gain by your labours.

49 TRANSFORMATION
Ke

The character of this hexagram is at one level a simple one, but complex in its depth. It shows an animal skin laid out to dry. Such a skin would have been the habitual garb of the shaman, a way in which his or her persona was taken over by the spirit of the animal, and thus of the gods/Heaven. Through wearing the hide, the person changes, but does so by disguise or by taking on another persona.

The trigrams are marsh above and fire below. Fire working on marsh causes the water to transform. But more important is the direct link between this hexagram and shamanistic practices.

FIRST NINE You can draw strength from a new infusion of energy and insight.

SECOND SIX No more hesitation.

THIRD NINE Think through everything that you are planning and only move ahead when you are really convinced.

FOURTH NINE Do not be deflected. Seize the moment and change even that which seems certain to oppose you.

FIFTH NINE Be brave; seek guidance, with a sense of confidence that whatever the answer, you can respond.

UPPER SIX Learn to change with the times but to keep yourself centred.

50 THE SACRIFICE
Ting

The pot or vessel of this hexagram is one of the beautiful bronze Shang dynasty pots with three legs. Covered with fabulous mouldings of abstract animals, these were highly prized offerings between rulers and to the gods. In particular they were used to hold food offerings made to the kingly ancestors and to Heaven. They were an intrinsic part of Chinese divination and worship. It was believed that food presented in the tripod pot was blessed and transformed into sacred food. The smells ascended to Heaven while the actual food was shared out with those who partook of the ritual.

The trigrams are fire above and wind below. The whole thrust of the hexagram is the interplay of powerful forces – the wind represents our prayers arising to the powerful realms of Heaven. It reminds us of our need to communicate with the Divine.

FIRST SIX In times of difficulty you may have to take drastic steps and overturn what has been.

SECOND NINE You are alright. Be still and await the outcome of others' actions, but do not get embroiled in them.

THIRD NINE Things are not as you expected. But this is all for the good.

FOURTH NINE This is a bad sign. Do nothing.

FIFTH SIX Power does not always lie with the most wealthy or beautiful. Listen to wise words, rather than be dazzled by glory.

UPPER NINE You are well cared for. Do not waste this.

51 TRAUMA
Chen

The two trigrams are the same, both thunder. It is therefore hardly surprising that this hexagram is the one for shock or trauma. It is the nature of a shock or trauma to shake us up and often into action. Yet in such reactions, so the opening text of the hexagram says, we should keep some sense of balance and be centred. The image of the frightening power of the trauma and the laughter of the leader, the fear for 100 miles around and the fact that not a drop of sacred wine is spilt, shows that the noble is alert to the shock but not fundamentally disturbed.

FIRST NINE Problems come and take us by surprise. Put them in context and learn to relax.

SECOND SIX You have suffered a major set-back. Meditate on what this could mean and try to put this in a much wider, more spiritual context.

THIRD SIX Take your courage in your hands and act as you see fit.

FOURTH NINE Disasters usually have fall-out, like landslips after storms. Brace yourself to endure what must come.

FIFTH SIX Troubles afflict you but you know what your true course is, for you have been on it for some time.

UPPER SIX Do not act when disturbed. Be calm, then act, even if this causes people to comment.

52 STILLING
Ken

The two trigrams are the same: mountain. The mountain in Chinese represents the place of retreat from the mundane, of communion with the divine and of openness to one's self. It is a place of meditation and of immortality, which carries with it in Chinese thought the notion of powerful magic, out of the body experiences, etc. It is strongly associated with certain types of shaman. This is therefore a very significant hexagram, stressing retreat from the mundane, and the ancient text makes this clear with what is essentially a description of the shaman who can travel out of his body.

First six Meditate.

Second six Just concentrating on your own state may prove useful to you but not to those around you who need guidance.

Third nine Withdrawing from ordinary life and trying to be spiritual by yourself is dangerous.

Fourth six Meditate.

Fifth six Think before you speak.

Upper nine Be still, listen and act then with integrity.

53 COASTING
Chien

The two trigrams are wind above and the mountain below. The character has the sign for water in it with the notion of water finding its way forward not by direct confrontation, but by gliding past. Given the frequency of the bird imagery in this hexagram, we have used the word 'coasting' to pick up on the idea of wind flowing over mountains which birds use for effortless travel to complement the water flowing image of the character. The whole emphasis of the hexagram is on flowing with, not struggling against or forcing the hand of nature/life.

First six Do not get out of your element. Stay where you are secure.

Second six Look for where you can be secure and at ease.

Third nine Shirking responsibilities and running away are not the answer. Face your troubles.

Fourth six Keep going, you are nearly within reach of your goal.

Fifth nine Seek help from the family or from Heaven and you will be able to overcome your frustrations.

Upper nine If you can sort out your own troubles and arrive somewhere where you feel secure, you will help others.

54 MARRYING THE YOUNGER SISTER
Kuei Mei

The trigrams are thunder above and marsh below. They are a volatile combination, each likely to produce shocks or to bog you down. This is the same with sorting out family affairs. This hexagram is rooted in Chinese feudal and patriarchal structures and concerns the problems of getting family relationships sorted out and of the tensions between those with power and those without.

FIRST NINE Things may not be as you planned, but you can still make a good life of where you have ended up.

SECOND NINE Act responsibly and seek counsel, especially from those who have suffered.

THIRD SIX You can expect gradual improvements.

FOURTH NINE Do not panic! Things will come right eventually.

FIFTH SIX It may seem that others have achieved their goal, but do not give up. Your time is coming.

UPPER SIX You have missed your opportunity. Do not go on striving for that which is past.

55 SOVEREIGNTY
Feng

The two trigrams are thunder above and fire below. The character shows a full wine cup and above it two sheaves of corn – like a cornucopia. It is the symbol of plenty and prosperity, and was also the name of the capital city of the Chou, the founding dynasty of the *I Ching*. This explains why the hexagram is very much concerned with the ruler, his powers and his fortune. This is effectively an imperial hexagram, indicating what a good ruler can expect.

FIRST NINE Look for those who can respond to you, even if for just a short time. This will help you act.

SECOND SIX You can see what others cannot see. Do not be impatient with them, but take your time to reveal to others what is obvious to you.

THIRD NINE Do not overdo it. You are trying for too much too quickly.

FOURTH NINE Guided by your vision, you need to find others who can share this if you are to succeed.

FIFTH SIX All will go well.

UPPER SIX You may have the external trappings of prosperity, but that does not mean that life is good. Open up to others and reveal yourself, not just your wealth or authority.

56 THE TRAVELLER
Lu

The two trigrams are fire above and mountain below. The whole thrust of this hexagram is that the traveller brings uncertainty yet has to be treated with respect. Hospitality was very important to early Chinese culture. The person who has seen the world brings unknown and dangerous ideas into enclosed societies, yet he must be respected for fear that he will return with enemies.

FIRST SIX Those who challenge us by questioning what we hold dear are disturbing, but may be right.

SECOND SIX Wealth is not everything.

THIRD NINE You are playing with fire. Beware.

FOURTH NINE Wealth and success bring fear.

FIFTH SIX You win some, you lose some.

UPPER NINE Be concerned for others and you will be alright. Mock others and this will rebound on you.

57 YIELDING
Sun

The two trigrams are the same: wind. Just as wind blows around, entering wherever it wills, so this hexagram combines the notion of yielding to the power of the wind with the idea of the wind penetrating. Actions should mirror this. They should be capable of moving things, but do so by gentle force which leads to yielding rather than violent force leading to resistance.

FIRST SIX Take stock of what is going on and seek advice.

SECOND NINE Seek advice from different sources to help you understand what is going on.

THIRD NINE There are times when you must stand up and be counted.

FOURTH SIX Take risks and go for more than you have done in the past.

FIFTH NINE Do not rush at things. Allow the winds of change to come, but be prepared.

UPPER NINE Beware, you are putting yourself at risk.

58 DELIGHT
Tui

The two trigrams are the same: marsh. This double water sign means fecundity, plenty and pleasure. This hexagram is one of the most cheerful and optimistic. Its character carries the connotation of both speech and of pleasure. It is a pun on the notion of the oracle speaking and bringing news of delight and happiness.

FIRST NINE Work together with others for that which is best and all will go well.

SECOND NINE No further commentary necessary.

THIRD SIX Trying too hard for something often destroys it.

FOURTH NINE Pleasure comes when you least expect it and not when you want it.

FIFTH NINE No further comment necessary.

UPPER SIX Do not be lured by pleasures, for they can be a trap.

UPPER NINE Enjoy your wine, but don't let it go to your head and give you false ideas of success or insight!

59 SCATTERING
Huan

The two trigrams are wind above and water below. They have the connotation of dispersal and of expansion. The wind and water carry things far away, with results which cannot be always determined. But water driven on by wind can also create floods. There is both potential and risk in this hexagram.

FIRST SIX Rely on those who have the strength to carry you through such a time.

SECOND NINE The actions necessary for a change can be very unpleasant. Be sure you know what you are doing.

THIRD SIX The consequences of your actions will affect you the most.

FOURTH SIX Breaking up an old group in order to be free to create a new one often takes less adventurous people by surprise. But this may be what you need to do.

FIFTH NINE Some actions have to be undertaken, no matter how difficult.

UPPER NINE You may have to leave your kith and kin for a while in order to resolve this crisis.

60 RESTRAINT
Chieh

The two trigrams are water above and marsh below. The character is interesting. It combines the sign for bamboo above and a phonetic sign below. Bamboo is seen in Chinese thought as a regulator, for its joints appear at regular intervals along the stem. By taking a natural instance of regulation, the hexagram is indicating that regulation or restraint is a natural part of life, and that as such it has a proper place and should not be overdone, nor overlooked.

FIRST NINE Do not make any big changes or undertake anything new.

SECOND NINE This is a time for you to act and to seize the moment.

THIRD SIX You know the rules. Do not try to break them.

FOURTH SIX What is most pleasing is that you act properly but without violence or violent intent.

FIFTH NINE Chose to act properly and you will be rewarded.

UPPER SIX Dictatorial behaviour is wrong, but all such rulers and rules eventually collapse.

61 KNOWING
Chung Fu

The two trigrams are wind above and marsh below. The whole emphasis of this hexagram is on the balancing of one's inner being with the demands of life. Throughout animal images are used, usually in a mixture of symbolic and actual ways. Thus in the opening ancient text, the reference to suckling pigs and

fish is both to having such a bounty of food and to fertility –
both being images of pregnancy and children. The second
character shows a hen covering her young ones.

FIRST NINE When circumstances offer a time of reflection on
the meaning and purpose of life, take it.

SECOND NINE You have a good life. Share what you have and
it will be even better.

THIRD SIX You cannot make up your mind. Now is not the
time to try and do so.

FOURTH SIX Changes happen, including loss. This is part of
life.

FIFTH NINE Opposition is now restrained. Do what is right.

UPPER NINE The cock call alarms the sun into daybreak
according to Chinese tradition. This way of proceeding may be
effective, but doesn't win friends.

62 THE SMALL THINGS
Hsiao Kuo

The trigrams are thunder above and mountain below. The
emphasis of this hexagram is on being modest in your
undertaking. There is an echo of the Icarus story in the bird
whose song should descend to Earth rather than soar to
Heaven. Minor problems, says the hexagram, you can tackle,
but don't overdo it. Moderation in all things.

FIRST SIX Stay put.

SECOND SIX Do not always assume that the most powerful
can help you. Perhaps those who are less powerful are your
real friends.

THIRD NINE Do not overstretch yourself or take on someone
who is frankly better prepared than you.

FOURTH NINE You know what you are capable of; don't
overdo it,' nor look for some excuse to do so.

FIFTH SIX There seem to be great possibilities, but in fact they
are worth nothing.

UPPER SIX You are being too extravagant in your aims. If you
don't temper these with some realism, you will suffer.

63 FINISHED
Chi Chi

The two trigrams are water above and fire below. The title is a joke! It is saying, here we are at the penultimate hexagram and we are telling you it's all over! It is making the point that the nature of the *I Ching* is change and thus it is appropriate that the penultimate reminds you that even when things seem finished – indeed, *are* finished – there is a new cycle just beginning. This is reinforced by the final hexagram, 'Unfinished'!

FIRST NINE Go slowly.

SECOND SIX Patience. What you are looking for will come in its own good time.

THIRD NINE What is being planned requires a true hero. Beware of undertaking something beyond your skills.

FOURTH SIX The situation is not good. Be careful.

FIFTH NINE Don't go by appearances, because Heaven knows what is true.

UPPER SIX Don't go beyond your depth.

64 UNFINISHED
Wei Chi

The two trigrams are fire above and water below. This hexagram continues the point made in 63 – namely, here we are at the end, but it is not the end, it is just the beginning...

This is picked up in the ancient text. Normally, any crossing of the river or stream in earlier hexagrams has been a straightforward instruction – 'Cross the great river', etc. Here, the fox is in the midst of doing so; the crossing is not yet completed. He is already in trouble and may never reach the other side. This is the heart of this whole hexagram.

FIRST SIX Things are a little out of control. Don't go on.

SECOND NINE Go slowly and things will resolve themselves.

THIRD SIX Finish what you are already involved in before making any major new decisions.

Fourth nine Things may seem chaotic and disturbed, but this is necessary to enable you to see the nature of the task before you.

Fifth six Be wise and be sincere. Anything less will be poor.

Upper nine Don't get carried away with success and power. This can lead you into very basic moral mistakes which then destroy what you have gained.

3
THE RADICALS

THE RADICALS

In preparing to work on the text, we looked in detail at the title characters of each hexagram. In a somewhat unconventional way, we broke them down in order to try and get inside the meaning of the characters.

Each Chinese character has one of 214 radicals as its basic component. By understanding what that radical itself means, you can often get a hint or suggestion of what the whole character might mean. Thus, for example, radical 149 means 'words' or 'talk'. When this forms part of other characters, you can be fairly sure that the character will have something to do with words, speech, insults and so forth.

Given the oracle bone origins of Chinese writing and of the *I Ching*, we felt it was worthwhile looking at the pictorial meanings which could be discerned within the characters. It has to be said that we did so in a mixed spirit of exploration, archaeology and fun, but the end results surprised both of us in terms of the insights which we gained and which so profoundly affected Jay's poems.

1 Ch'ien

A, the character for '10', a perfect, complete and mystical number, is repeated twice, around B, which stands for 'day' = the perfect beginning to the day, sunrise at the beginning of time. This is further enhanced by C, the character for 'the primal, the first, One'.

2 K'un

A is 'earth' or 'ground' and in the Chinese Triad of Heaven, Earth and humanity, Earth is yin – female. B is the character for 'reporting to the centre, to the middle'.

3 Chun

The radical A stands for 'a plant sprouting' and here it means new birth pushing up through the ground.

4 Meng

A is the character for 'grass', while B is made up of two elements, 'a roof' with 'piglets' under it, the meaning of which is 'home'.

5 Hsu

A is 'rain' and B means 'again'. Yet more rain!

6 *Sung*

A, 'word, speech', combined with B, meaning 'public, open' = speaking out.

7 *Shih*

A means 'lots of people' while B means 'to circle' or 'to cap'. Lots of people going round and round wearing caps – the army!

8 *Pi*

This character is in fact a radical of its own, but we have broken it down, using a certain degree of licence! A is 'up' and B could be 'seven', a magical number of great power. Thus we have the sense of everything coming together and going up. Unity.

9 *Hsiao Ch'u*

Two characters here:

i) This means 'small, mean, petty'.

ii) Means 'domestic' – having the sign for 'field' at its base, with the notion of that which is at hand, homely.

10 *Li*

An interesting one, for A means 'a corpse' while B means 'return' = bringing back either the dead or from the dead.

11 *T'ai*

A is the sign for 'water' and B seems to indicate 'a bearer, someone carrying' – hence the water bearer.

12 *P'i*

A very clear one here, for A means 'not' and B 'open mouth'. Silence of the unopened mouth.

13 *T'ung Jen*

Two characters:

i) 'The open mouth', contained within a border meaning 'togetherness'.
ii) This is the radical for 'man, person'.

14 *Ta Yu*

Two characters:

i) 'Great, big, many'.
ii) 'To have, to hold'.

Hence, many possessions.

15 *Ch'ien*

A, 'word' or 'speech', combined with B, meaning 'to unite, to connect, to be equal to each other' = those who are connected, guided by the Word.

16 *Yü*

A means 'a young person', usually a son, while B is adapted from the character for 'home'. The young people living at home, full of enthusiasm.

17 *Sui*

A means 'fertile' while B we have broken down into its base, which is the radical for 'walking' (i) or 'path' and the radical for 'moon' (ii), hence the notion of being led by the moonlight along a path.

18 *Ku*

Interesting one, for A means 'worm' and here we have three of them, crawling over B, the character for 'a tool'. The sense is of decay.

19 *Lin*

A is the character for 'a leader', while B is the sign for 'a roof'. C consists of three open mouths. We read this as the leader seeking to bring some order or unity to the diverse opinions in his group.

20 *Kuan*

A means 'compassion and concern', while B is the sign for 'looking, seeing'. Thus, to look with compassion. This is the character which is the first part of the name of the most popular figure in Chinese belief, the goddess of compassion, Kuan Yin. Hence Jay's deliberate use of yin in his title.

21 *Shi Ho*

Two characters, both with A, the radical for 'mouth', dominant:

i) B = the character for 'bamboo', hence chewing on bamboo.
ii) 'To finish, to leave'.

22 *Pi*

A, the sign for 'grasses', combined with B, 'cowrie shells', which were one of the world's oldest forms of currency, hence the meaning 'valuable and expensive'.

23 *Po*

A symbolizes 'the knife' and dominates this character.

24 *Fu*

A = 'to step out with the left foot', B = 'day', C = 'culture' (meant in the broadest sense). Hence to go back to your own folk, your own kind.

25 *Wu Wang*

Two characters:

i) This is the radical for 'not' or 'without'.
ii) A means 'absent', while B means 'woman'.

Thus, 'the not absent woman' or the one who stays.

26 *Ta Chu*

Two characters:

i) This is the radical for 'great, big, many'.
ii) 'Domestic'.

This is a big version of no.9, where the same second character appears.

27 *I*

A means 'a scholar, official', but we also saw it as being the shape of the jaws around the mouth. B means 'a leaf of a book, a page'. Hence the notion of devouring the book, which is what a scholar does but what the jaws working on a mouthful of words also do.

28 *Ta Kuo*

Two characters:

i) 'Great, big, many'.
ii) A is the sign for 'walking, travelling', while B means 'a desert'.

Jay has given this the powerful title of Exodus. Travelling through a great desert, a time of trial and endurance.

29 *Kan*

A means 'earth', while B means 'lack of'. A powerfully negative way to describe the fearfulness of water, deep water – bottomless, without earth or ground.

30 *Li*

A very complex character with interesting levels of meaning within it. A means 'above', B means 'evil, malignant', while C means 'a footprint'. D is a very complicated character in terms of its meaning. It means 'a bright bird', a magnificent creature who rises with the brightness of the sun. It forms part of the character of the phoenix. Thus we have the image of this brilliant bright bird of the sun and rebirth soaring above the evil and malignant impressions of the past – the footprint.

31 *Hsian*

A, the radical here, is 'mouth', combined with B, the notion of 'peoples', giving the idea of a united voice for all people.

32 *Heng*

A is the radical for 'heart', combined with B, meaning 'extreme, limit'. The heart is going to the limit, the limits of commitment.

33 *Tun*

A is 'walk' or 'journey', with B meaning 'the moon' and C 'pig', a symbol which also carries with it the connotation of 'domestic, homely – the farm'. Hence the journey by moonlight to home.

34 *Ta Chuang*

Two characters:

i) 'Big, great, many'.
ii) A means 'a split tree' or 'a bed', while B means 'a scholar'.

Is it that the scholar draws strength from reclining or from the heart of the split tree?

35 *Chin*

A little imaginative work here, for we see A as being based upon the character for 'two' and this being repeated by the inner symbols, meaning 'to follow one after another'. B means 'day'.

36 *Ming I*

Two characters:

i) A means 'the sun' while B means 'the moon'. Together they mean 'luminous brightness' as well as 'being clever'.
ii) A fascinating image, for it contains the symbol for 'a bow', which I have circled, with the symbol for 'a great man' behind it. The dimming is apparently done by this man with a bow. This evoked the greatest of all Chinese ancient myths, the legend of Yi the Archer. The world was threatened by seven suns which were drying up the water, withering the crops and slaying the people. The greatest archer in the world, Yi, was called upon to deal with them. With his bow he downed six of the suns, which turned out to be evil forces in the shape of crows. Finally only the true sun was left, sufficient in its warmth and light.

37 *Chia Jen*

Two characters:

i) This character means 'family' and shows piglets under the roof.
ii) The radical for 'man'.

The family based around a man, yet interestingly linked here to the oracle about the shaman woman.

38 *Kuei*

A, 'eyes', combined with B, meaning 'back to back' and C, 'Heaven'. Are you yearning to see Heaven, but looking backwards?

39 *Chien*

A, 'roof', B 'eight' and C 'foot' or 'enough'. This one left us unsure of its meaning.

40 *Chiai*

A character full of symbols of sharpness. A means 'a horn', while B is 'a knife', combined with C, which is 'a war axe', a wicked blade mounted upon an eight foot staff. The character is about cutting loose, penetrating.

41 *Sun*

A, 'power' or 'force', with B, 'mouth' and C, 'wealth'.

42 I

A is the symbol for 'a tool', but what B is we could not discover.

43 Kuai

This character has lost a radical for 'water' over the centuries. It used to be combined with B, which means 'divide'. So we have water dividing, forking, branching.

44 Kou

A, 'woman', B, 'mouth', C, 'strength'. This is a powerful and sensual woman, but with something foreboding about her.

45 Tsui

A, 'grass', with B, 'above', and then C, 'follow', with D, '10'. It seems to speak of the leader followed by the hosts across the plains.

46 Sheng

A, 'men', B, '10'.

47 K'un

A is 'a tree' within B, 'a border' or 'country'.

48 Ching

This is an actual pictogram, for it shows a well in the centre of a set of field boundaries.

49 Ke

A is a very ancient sign for 'an animal skin drying' and B is the sign for 'middle'. A skin drying in the middle of the day's heat and thus changing into leather?

50 Ting

A is 'an eye' over B, which is either 'a bed and a splinter' or 'two split tree trunks'. However, there is another image here. It could well be an actual pictogram of a sacrificial cooking pot on a tripod of legs.

51 *Chen*

A is 'rain', with B being 'a cave' and C 'possessions' or 'culture'. Is this the notion of threat to your security through the wild forces of nature?

52 *Ken*

This one defeated us!

53 *Chien*

A is the sign for 'water' with B being the symbol for 'a waggon' or transport of some kind and C is 'piercing, penetrating'. The imagery here is of the free-flowing and penetrating nature of water – a frequent Chinese and especially Taoist image – which moves all before it like a waggon.

54 *Kuei Mei*

Two characters:

i) A is 'the foot on the ground, earthed'. B is 'caps on heads'.
ii) A is 'woman', combined with B, 'a sage' or 'wise one'.

55 Feng

This is effectively a cornucopia, with A, 'a basket of grain', on top of B, 'a wine cup'.

56 Lu

A is a complex character which has the connotation of 'square' or 'being morally just and squared' and of being 'a road or path to follow'. B means 'to diverge, to go off at another angle'. This fits the traveller, the one who follows his own righteous path – one which cuts across the path of the mighty and stands in contradiction.

57 Sun

A is the character for 'a seal', repeated, meaning 'binding'. B is the character for 'all together'.

58 Tui

A means 'fun, enjoyment' and B is 'a mouth on legs' – an oracle that travels, dances and enjoys itself!

59 Huan

A is the sign for 'water', B is 'the horn' and C is 'cutting'. Like water, this is a character meaning free flowing, cutting through all that obscures or restrains.

60 Chieh

A is the sign for 'bamboo', with B being a phonetic sign emphasizing the sound. The bamboo is depicted as regular notches for one of its key features is the equal distance between the notes in its stem. A sign of measurement and regulation.

61 *Chung Fu*
Two characters:

i) 'Middle'.
ii) A is the sign of 'a hen', with B being the sign for 'child', hence a broody hen.

62 *Hsiao Kuo*
Two characters:

i) 'Small'.
ii) A, 'walk' or 'journey', with B, 'desert'.

A small but difficult journey.

63 *Chi Chi*
Two characters:

i) This consists of A, 'sunset', over B, 'seven', with the character for 'primary, original, first'.
ii) A is for 'water', B seems to have some aspect of fire within it and C is 'the moon'.

64 *Wei Chi*
Two characters:

i) 'Not yet'.
ii) A is 'water', combined with B, encapsulating 'fire', over C, 'the moon'.

Exercise

CRACKING THE BONE

Martin Palmer

When Jay and I were exploring the divinatory origins of the *I Ching*, I was anxious to show how random cracks on a shell or bone produced by the application of heat had become Chinese written characters.

To illustrate how this worked, we invented this exercise and what follows is a record of the 'reading' or 'oracle' that we produced. We recommend that you try this as well.

We started with a question which Jay framed in his mind but did not tell me. His question, a classic one, was 'Should we move the capital city?'

Meanwhile, I drew a completely random set of lines on a sheet of paper *(see figure opposite)* – the sort of lines that appear on the oracle bones, plus a bit of artistic licence!

Then I asked Jay, mindful of his enquiry about moving the capital city, to 'read' the squiggles I had made in two sets of four. He read:

1. A. Snake. B. Gap over a river. C. Cross falling into the depths. D. Decline.
2. A. Centre of a lake. B. Dispersal. C. Ascent from the centre (falling away). D. Rooting in earth.

Jay then reworked these two sets of 'images' into two messages. They gave him:

1. The snake falls into the depths. Decline.
2. The centre falls away and then ascends and is re-rooted. New beginning.

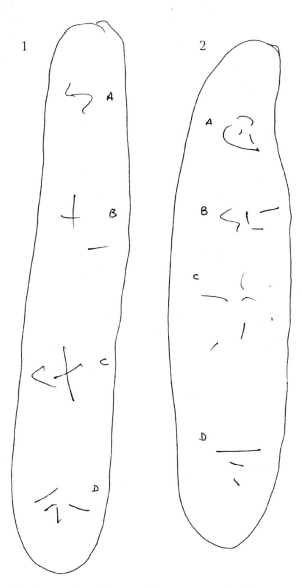

Thus his 'answer' to his question seems to indicate a move of the capital city and a new beginning.

By such an exercise it is possible to see how perceived images and pictures in the cracks began to give rise to Chinese pictographic writing. It is also quite fun to do!

We are making no great claims for this exercise, but it does give those who use it a feeling for the methods by which the oracles of the *I Ching* were given.

Terracotta warriors and horses positioned to protect the tomb of the first Emperor of China c.210 BC. Intended to protect him for thousands of years, they were destroyed within seven years of the Emperor's death.